REVISITING
MARY
HIGGINS
CLARK

Critical Companions to Popular Contemporary Writers
Second Series

Isabel Allende *by Karen Castellucci Cox*

Julia Alvarez *by Silvio Sirias*

Rudolfo A. Anaya *by Margarite Fernandez Olmos*

Maya Angelou *by Mary Jane Lupton*

Ray Bradbury *by Robin Anne Reid*

Louise Erdrich *by Lorena L. Stookey*

Ernest J. Gaines *by Karen Carmean*

Gabriel García Márquez *by Rubén Pelayo*

Kaye Gibbons *by Mary Jean DeMarr*

John Irving *by Josie P. Campbell*

Garrison Keillor *by Marcia Songer*

Jamaica Kincaid *by Lizabeth Paravisini-Gebert*

Revisiting Stephen King *by Sharon A. Russell*

Barbara Kingsolver *by Mary Jean DeMarr*

Maxine Hong Kingston *by E. D. Huntley*

Terry McMillan *by Paulette Richards*

Larry McMurtry *by John M. Reilley*

Toni Morrison *by Missy Dehn Kubitschek*

Walter Mosley *by Charles E. Wilson, Jr.*

Gloria Naylor *by Charles E. Wilson, Jr.*

Chaim Potok *by Sanford Sternlicht*

Amy Tan *by E. D. Huntley*

Anne Tyler *by Paul Bail*

Leon Uris *by Kathleen Shine Cain*

Kurt Vonnegut *by Thomas F. Marvin*

Tom Wolfe *by Brian Abel Ragen*

REVISITING MARY HIGGINS CLARK

A Critical Companion

Linda De Roche

CRITICAL COMPANIONS TO POPULAR CONTEMPORARY WRITERS
Kathleen Gregory Klein, Series Editor

Greenwood Press
Westport, Connecticut • London

Library of Congress Cataloging-in-Publication Data

De Roche, Linda.
　Revisiting Mary Higgins Clark : a critical companion / Linda De Roche.
　　　p. cm.—(Critical companions to popular contemporary writers, ISSN 1082–4979)
　Includes bibliographical references and index.
　ISBN 0–313–32039–X (alk. paper)
　　1. Clark, Mary Higgins—Criticism and interpretation.　2. Detective and mystery
　stories, American—History and criticism.　I. Title.　II. Series.
　PS3553.L287Z66 2003
　813′.54—dc21　　　2002044847

British Library Cataloguing in Publication Data is available.

Library of Congress Catalog Card Number: 2002044847
ISBN: 0–313–32039–X
ISSN: 1082–4979

First published in 2003

Praeger Publishers, 88 Post Road West, Westport, CT 06881
An imprint of Greenwood Publishing Group, Inc.
www.praeger.com

Printed in the United States of America

The paper used in this book complies with the
Permanent Paper Standard issued by the National
Information Standards Organization (Z39.48–1984).

10　9　8　7　6　5　4　3　2　1

To Stéphane
Mon ami, mon amour
Pour toujours

Contents

Contents

Series Foreword

The authors who appear in the series Critical Companions to Popular Contemporary Writers are all best-selling writers. They do not simply have one successful novel, but a string of them. Fans, critics, and specialist readers eagerly anticipate their next book. For some, high cash advances and breakthrough sales figures are automatic; movie deals often follow. Some writers become household names, recognized by almost everyone.

But, their novels are read one by one. Each reader chooses to start and, more importantly, to finish a book because of what she or he finds there. The real test of a novel is in the satisfaction its readers experience. This series acknowledges the extraordinary involvement of readers and writers in creating a best-seller.

The authors included in this series were chosen by an Advisory Board composed of high school English teachers and high school and public librarians. They ranked a list of best-selling writers according to their popularity among different groups of readers. For the first series, writers in the top-ranked group who had received no book-length, academic, literary analysis (or none in at least the last ten years) were chosen. Because of this selection method, Critical Companions to Popular Contemporary Writers meets a need that is being addressed nowhere else. The success of these volumes as reported by reviewers, librarians, and teachers led to an expansion of the series mandate to include some writers with wide

critical attention—Toni Morrison, John Irving, and Maya Angelou, for example—to extend the usefulness of the series.

The volumes in the series are written by scholars with particular expertise in analyzing popular fiction. These specialists add an academic
focus to the popular success that these writers already enjoy.

The series is designed to appeal to a wide range of readers. The general
reading public will find explanations for the appeal of these well-known
writers. Fans will find biographical and fictional questions answered. Stu-
dents will find literary analysis, discussions of fictional genres, carefully
organized introductions to new ways of reading the novels, and bibliog-
raphies for additional research. Whether browsing through the book for
pleasure or using it for an assignment, readers will find that the most
recent novels of the authors are included.

Each volume begins with a biographical chapter drawing on published
information, autobiographies or memoirs, prior interviews, and, in some
cases, interviews given especially for this series. A chapter on literary
history and genres describes how the author's work fits into a larger literary context. The following chapters analyze the writer's most important,
most popular, and most recent novels in detail. Each chapter focuses on
one or more novels. This approach, suggested by the Advisory Board as
the most useful to student research, allows for an in-depth analysis of the
writer's fiction. Close and careful readings with numerous examples show
readers exactly how the novels work. These chapters are organized
around three central elements: plot development (how the story line
moves forward), character development (what the reader knows of the
important figures), and theme (the significant ideas of the novel). Chapters
may also include sections on generic conventions (how the novel is similar
to or different from others in its same category of science fiction, fantasy,
thriller, etc.), narrative point of view (who tells the story and how), symbols and literary language, and historical or social context. Each chapter
ends with an "alternative reading" of the novel. The volume concludes
with a primary and secondary bibliography, including reviews.

The alternative readings are a unique feature of this series. By demonstrating a particular way of reading each novel, they provide a clear example of how a specific perspective can reveal important aspects of the
book. In the alternative reading sections, one contemporary literary theory—such as feminist criticism, Marxism, new historicism, deconstruc-
tion, or Jungian psychological critique—is defined in brief, easily
comprehensible language. That definition is then applied to the novel to
highlight specific features that might go unnoticed or be understood dif-

ferently in a more general reading. Each volume defines two or three specific theories, making them part of the reader's understanding of how diverse meanings may be constructed from a single novel.

Taken collectively, the volumes in the Critical Companions to Popular Contemporary Writers series provide a wide-ranging investigation of the complexities of current best-selling fiction. By treating these novels seriously as both literary works and publishing successes, the series demonstrates the potential of popular literature in contemporary culture.

Kathleen Gregory Klein
Southern Connecticut State University

Acknowledgments

I count myself fortunate in friends. In fact, completing this book without them would have been impossible. So thanks and love to Susan Bentley, Marie Cusick, Betsy Nielsen, and Debbie Rickard for all the heart-to-hearts. Thanks as well to Lou Jeffries, librarian at The Hill School, not only for research assistance but also for moral support.

I am also grateful to Mary Higgins Clark and her publicist, Ms. Lisl Cade, for their assistance with my study.

To my husband Stéphane, I owe too much for words. He makes all things possible. This book is proof.

The Plot of Her Story

In May 1997, Mary Higgins Clark, the best-selling mystery and suspense writer, returned to her alma mater to address the graduates at Fordham University's 152nd commencement exercises. During her remarks, she offered them advice about what she called the "personal suspense novels" they had just begun to write. "The plot is what you will do for the rest of your life, and you are the protagonist," she told her audience ("Writer Says" 31)—and she should know. She has been devising plots, including the plot of her own story, since she was a young girl. While her own plot has had nearly as many twists and turns as the story lines of some of her novels, Clark, like her intrepid heroines, has gamely negotiated them all. Today, in fact, they give shape to her imaginary plots, for as she notes, "You always do put something of yourself in your work" (Stasio, "Dressed to Kill" 27).

Born in New York City on 24 December 1929, Mary Higgins grew up in the Bronx, where her father, Luke Joseph Higgins, an Irish immigrant, owned the Higgins Bar and Grille. Clark recalls her early childhood with fondness, particularly the family gatherings at which she and a host of aunts, great-aunts, and cousins, first- and second-generation descendants of her Irish grandparents, sat about the table spinning tales that made the world magical to an imaginative young girl. When she was ten years old, however, Clark's carefree childhood ended abruptly. She returned from early Mass one morning to learn that her beloved father had died in his sleep.

Burdened by debt, Clark's mother, Nora C. (Durkin) Higgins, who had been a bridal buyer at Manhattan's B. Altman department store prior to her marriage, was left with $2,000 to raise two sons and a daughter. The "enterprising" woman rented rooms in the family home (Kuczynski C1) and worked at a series of menial jobs to support her family. As Clark recalls, "We had no money after my father died, but we were always well dressed because Mother knew how to work the sales racks in the Fifth Avenue stores" (Stasio, "Dressed to Kill" 27). Her mother's ability to cope with tragedy taught Clark resilience and resourcefulness, two qualities that characterize her own heroines.

To contribute to the family's income, Mary worked as a babysitter and switchboard operator during high school. Following graduation from Villa Maria Academy, she postponed college to take a secretarial course and worked for several years as an advertising assistant at Remington Rand. One day, however, she abandoned her life's safe predictability after a friend, a Pan Am stewardess, casually remarked, "God, it was beastly hot in Calcutta." Those seven words opened up the world for Clark (Freeman 229). Signing on as a Pan Am stewardess, Mary was soon flying to exotic locales. She was also having some frightening adventures. "I was in a revolution in Syria," explains Clark, "and on the last flight into Czechoslovakia before the Iron Curtain went down" (Clark, "Interrogating Mary").

One year after her adventures had begun, Mary traded her wings for a wedding band, marrying Warren Clark, her brother's friend, on whom she had had a crush since she was sixteen years old, on December 26, 1949. She and her husband, who worked in the airline industry, settled in the Stuyvesant Town section of New York City to raise the three daughters and two sons who soon filled their house and lives. The busy mother began as well her quest to become a writer.

Enrolling in a creative writing course at New York University, Clark followed the advice of her professor to "write about what you know" (Freeman 231). Drawing on her experience as a stewardess on the last flight into Czechoslovakia, she began her first story, "Stowaway." Six years and forty rejection slips later, Clark sold it to *Extension* magazine for $100. When she telephoned her mother to share the news of her success, the ever-practical woman advised her daughter to bank her earnings. Mary, however, informed her that she intended to spend the money and to write other stories, to which her mother responded, "But, Mary, you've used up your idea" (Hoopes 53). Indeed, she had not.

In fact, Mary Higgins Clark had been preparing for a writing career since those childhood days of family storytelling, when she listened intently and absorbed all she heard. Soon she was putting to use what she had learned. At pajama parties, Clark has confided, "I would tell stories that began: 'Someone—or something—is standing behind that curtain, watching. And his—or its—eyes will fall on one of us. I wonder which one . . .'" (Hoopes 53). She had also begun to keep a diary when she was seven years old. Her first written effort, a poem, had been soundly praised by her mother, "who thought it was beautiful and made me recite it for everyone who came in," Clark recalls. She also wrote plays, which she forced her brothers to perform with her, reserving the starring role for herself (Fakih 36). "I loved to tell stories," Clark has confessed. "It was part of my Irish heritage" (Donohue 2). Throughout the years of her marriage, Clark continued to write stories for national magazines; then, in 1963, the short story market "absolutely went sour." *Collier's* and *Woman's Home Companion* ceased publication, and *Saturday Evening Post* abandoned short stories. "I'm not a *New Yorker* writer," notes Clark, ". . . so that was when I started writing radio shows" (Fakih 36).

The collapse of the short story market, however, was not the only impetus propelling Clark toward a new career. Diagnosed in 1959 with severe angina, Warren Clark suffered a series of heart attacks, and the couple lived the next five years "knowing there was an ax over his head" (Hubbard and McNeil). In 1964, Warren Clark suffered a fourth and fatal heart attack, and suddenly Mary found herself in the same situation that her mother had faced years before. Because Warren's heart condition had made him uninsurable, Clark was left an impoverished young widow, with five children between the ages of five and thirteen depending upon her. Recognizing that she could not support her family on the income of a freelance writer, she took a full-time job writing radio scripts. She never abandoned her dream of establishing herself as a writer, however, rising early each morning to write for two hours before the children awakened at 7:00 A.M.

One of Clark's first radio assignments was writing biographical sketches about historical figures for a weekday program called *Portrait of a Patriot*. This "three-year tutorial in history," as Clark calls it (Fakih 36), led inevitably to a biographical novel as her first attempt at full-length fiction. Published in 1969, *Aspire to the Heavens,* based on the life of George Washington, gave little indication of Clark's future direction as a writer or of the success she would achieve. It was a "commercial disaster and remaindered as it came off the press," notes Clark. The novel has had a second life, however, following its publication in 2002 as *Mount Vernon Love Story: A Novel of George and Martha Washington*. Despite its initial failure, "it showed," Clark asserts, "that I could write a book and get it published" (Clark, "Interrogating Mary"). Nevertheless, the novel's dismal failure did not signal a brilliant writing career, and its second life owes as much to Clark's remarkable popularity as to its literary merit.

Clark's stint as a radio scriptwriter and eventually, when she and a partner created Aerial Communications in 1970, as a producer, lasted fourteen years and served to some extent as her writing apprenticeship. Producing and writing shows on a variety of topics, from fashion to crime prevention, Clark sharpened her skills. In fact, the demands of radio scriptwriting, especially its fast pacing and believable dialogue, were important to her future in novels. Writing for the radio, notes Kimberly Olson Fakih, also helped her to learn "to compress vast amounts of information (or clues) into dense, well-paced segments." As Clark herself has noted, "When you have a four-minute program, you learn to write succinctly. . . . Suspense also must move quickly" (Fakih 36).

Despite the fate of her first novel, Clark was determined to succeed. She turned her attention to her own bookshelf as she cast about for a story idea. "I was astonished to realize," she observed," that ninety percent of the books I'd read in the last couple of years had been mysteries ("Storyteller" 10). After some additional "soul-digging," Clark began to name her favorite authors, a list that included Mary Roberts Rinehart, Josephine Tey, Agatha Christie, and Charlotte Armstrong. "That was the clue," she realized, "that helped me decide to try a suspense novel" ("Storyteller" 10). In writing about what she knew best, Mary Higgins Clark would finally find success.

Clark's interest in sleuthing and the dark underside of life had begun, she recalls, in childhood, with the Bobbsey Twins books and the Lindbergh baby kidnapping. She remembers especially the "wonderful solution" (Fakih 36) to the mystery that formed the plot of *The Bobbsey Twins and the Baby May*. In that tale, the Bobbseys find an infant abandoned on their doorstep at the same time that an old woman begins to prowl about their home. The twins discover that the old woman, who had just recovered from temporary amnesia, had been the baby's nurse. "A can of soup had hit her on the head and she had forgotten the baby. Once she remembered," notes Clark, "she tries to steal the baby back" (Fakih 36). It was, of course, a perfectly reasonable solution to the Bobbseys' puzzle.

Clark recalls as well the haunting power of the Lindbergh baby kidnapping in the 1920s. Long after the event, her parents never let her forget that the kidnappers had deposited their ransom note close to the family's summer cottage, which was located near the Throgs Neck Bridge, the tip of the Bronx on Long Island Sound. Each time they passed St. Raymond's Cemetery on their way to their summer retreat, Clark's father reminded his children that at the flower shop across the street from St. Raymond's "the note for that little baby was left" (Fakih 36). From such beginnings was born a writer who, by her own admission, "can't balance a checkbook, but [who] can juggle clues in [her] head" (Hoopes 54).

In 1975, Clark demonstrated her talent for juggling clues in the novel that became her first best-seller, *Where Are the Children?*. With its vulnerable heroine and endangered children, the tightly plotted narrative tapped its readers' most basic fears. The tense and fast-paced novel of mystery and suspense, which, according to Clark, took her "a year and a half to write and another year and a half to rewrite" (Donohue 2), climbed quickly on the best-seller lists and is now in its seventieth printing. Three years later, by the time she had published *A Stranger Is Watching,* Clark had abandoned her radio business to her partner to devote herself full time to writing novels. Today those works have made her one of the most successful popular contemporary writers. Testament to her success is the $64 million contract that Clark signed with her publisher, Simon and Schuster, on the twenty-fifth anniversary of their partnership in April 2000 ("Pen Pals" B2). Perhaps the best measure of the degree to which Clark's novels touch her readers, however, is the fact that she frequently and simultaneously tops both the hardcover and paperback *New York Times* best-seller lists. Her novels may not earn critical accolades, but to her many fans, who eagerly await publication of each new tale, she is the unrivalled "Queen of Suspense."

The success of *Where Are the Children?* provided the widowed mother of five with the financial security to educate not only her children but also herself. In 1974, Clark began to pursue the college degree she had deferred for marriage. In 1979, the forty-nine-year-old author graduated summa cum laude with a bachelor of arts degree in philosophy from Fordham University. Nine years later, she received an honorary doctorate from her alma mater; later she served on its board of trustees. She holds seventeen other honorary doctorates. Education has always been important to Mary Higgins Clark, as the invitation to her graduation party testified. On the card Clark had printed, "This invitation is 25 years overdue—help prove it's not too late" (Clark, "Interrogating Mary").

A disciplined writer who once told her audience at a public lecture on "Suspense Writing: From Creation to Publication" that "you must keep honing your craft" (Donohue 2), Clark takes her work seriously. Writing, she explains, is "a real job": "I write all day; I don't have lunch out. If you work everyday, at the end of the year you have a book" (Donohue 2). Such a routine accounts for the nineteen best-selling novels of mystery and suspense, the three short story collections, the four Christmas novels, and the memoir, *Kitchen Privileges* (2002), that she has published since the first bestseller in 1975.

Several of those works, including *A Stranger Is Watching* and *Where Are the Children?*, have been made into feature films. Others, such as *The Cradle Will Fall*, *A Cry in the Night* (which featured Clark's daughter Carol in the lead role), *Stillwatch*, *While My Pretty One Sleeps*, *Remember Me*, and two stories from *The Anastasia Syndrome and Other Stories*, became television films. Telemovies of Clark's novels, in fact, seem set to be a regular feature. PAX TV, the family entertainment broadcast network, began airing the first of six original made-for-PAX mystery movies, *Loves Music, Loves to Dance*, in February 2002. It will be followed by productions of *Pretend You Don't See Her*, the short story "Lucky Day," *You Belong to Me*, "Haven't We Met Before," and *All Around the Town*. Clark made cameo appearances in both *While My Pretty One Sleeps* and *Remember Me*, but readers have nothing to fear. She has no intention of abandoning her pen for greasepaint.

Clark has, however, recently ventured into new publishing territory. In April 2000, Simon and Schuster released an electronic version of her then current bestseller, *Before I Say Good-Bye*, as well as nine of her other novels, making them available for laptop and desktop computers, electronic reading devices, and personal digital assistants (Kuczynski C1). The success of the venture is uncertain, but it certainly has the potential of increasing her audience—not that she necessarily needs it. Her books already sell well, even in European countries such as the Netherlands, Italy, Great Britain, and Germany. In fact, she is the best-selling fiction author in France, where, according to John Baker of *Publishers Weekly*, "they name streets after her" (Kuczynski C17).

Accolades, of course, have certainly come Clark's way. In 1980, she received France's Grand Prix de Littérature Policière, further evidence of her long-standing Gallic appeal. The French renewed their love affair with Clark in 1998, when she received The Literary Award at the Deauville Film Festival, and in 2000, when the French minister of culture named her "Chevalier of the Order of Arts and Letters." Twice her Irish heritage, in which she takes great pride, considering it an important influence on her writing, has led to honor: In 1992, she was named the Irish Woman of the Year by the Irish-American Heritage and Cultural Week Committee of the

Board of Education of the City of New York; the following year, the American-Irish Historical Society awarded her its Gold Medal of Honor. Among other awards, Clark also received the National Arts Club's first Gold Medal in Education in 1994, tribute to her advocacy of literacy and to her example of lifelong learning. Her 1997 Horatio Alger Award also testifies to her life of achievement. Active in Catholic affairs, Clark was made a Dame of the Order of St. Gregory the Great, a papal honor. She is also a Dame of Malta and a Lady of the Holy Sepulchre of Jerusalem. The range of these awards, as well as others, including the Passionists' Ethics in Literature Award in 2002, testifies positively to both Clark's personal and her professional habits of mind and being.

Despite her disciplined writing schedule, Clark devotes both time and talent to professional organizations and colleagues. She has served on the board of directors and as president of the Mystery Writers of America and as chairwoman of the International Crime Writers Congress. She is also an active member of the Society of Magazine Writers and Journalists. In 2000, Clark was chosen by the Mystery Writers of America as Grand Master of the Edgar Awards, and an annual Mary Higgins Clark Award sponsored by Simon and Schuster, to be given to authors of suspense fiction writing in the Mary Higgins Clark tradition, was launched by the Mystery Writers of America during Edgars week in 2001. Clark is also a founding member of the Adams Round Table, a group of writers that has included Thomas Chastain, Dorothy Salisbury Davis, Justin Scott, Mickey Friedman, Susan Isaacs, and Whitley Strieber. At monthly meetings, members discuss their craft and plot their murders. Occasionally they even collaborate, publishing story collections that include *Missing in Manhattan* (1992) and *Murder in the Family* (2002). In support of her mystery-writing colleagues, Clark also launched the *Mary Higgins Clark Mystery Magazine* in 1996 to provide a forum for short fiction. She has also edited, in cooperation with the International Association of Crime Writers, a collection of twenty-two short stories, including works by P. D. James and Sara Paretsky, entitled *Bad Behavior: Mystery Stories* (1995), as well as *The Plot Thickens* (1997) and the Mystery Writers of America anthology *The Night Awakens* (2000). Pleased that other female suspense writers are enjoying success—"There's more room for us today," she observes—Clark cites Sue Grafton and Patricia Cornwell among her favorite contemporary writers of the genre (Toepfer, "Clean-Cut" 36).

A friend of libraries, Clark has been active in Literacy Volunteers, writing and speaking on behalf of the organization. In fact, she and the other members of the Adams Round Table donated the publisher's advance for one of their story collections to the organization. As Clark says, "I don't think it's right for writers to ignore the people who can't read!" (O'Neill 65).

Until 1996, Clark, a resident of Saddle River, New Jersey, and New York City, had enjoyed the life of "an aging debutante. I have three buddies, all widows," observed the long-widowed writer in an interview, "and we go on trips together" (Toepfer, "Clean-Cut" 36). Less than six months after this interview, however, she was walking down the aisle for a third trip to the altar. (A six-year second marriage to lawyer Ray Ploetz, which Clark calls "a colossal mistake" (Hubbard and McNeil), ended in annulment in 1986.) On 30 November 1996, the sixty-seven-year-old mystery writer married John Conheeney, a retired chief executive officer of Merrill Lynch Futures Inc. Theirs was a match engineered by Clark's youngest daughter, Patricia Derenzo, an executive assistant at the New York Mercantile Exchange.

Clark recalls that Patty, even at age five, was intent on playing match-maker for her mother. Not long after her father's death in 1964, the little girl had offered the postman a pair of her father's pajamas and invited him "to stay the night." "Patty proposed to everyone," Clark observes. "She wanted a man in the house." When Patty met Conheeney, whose wife of forty years had died of cancer in 1994, "My heart told me they'd be perfect together," she claims. Patty encouraged her mother to invite the former Wall Street executive to her 1996 St. Patrick's Day celebration, and Conheeney, who had read several of Clark's novels and feared that "she was too sophisticated for me" (Hubbard and McNeil), accepted. By June, the couple was engaged; in November they married. Following a reception at which the newlyweds danced long into the night, Patty observed, "They are like teenagers in love" ("Mary Higgins Clark & John Conheeney" 80). Readers of her 1996 collection of short stories, *My Gal Sunday*, a work that conveys the joy of new love and the satisfactions of marital bliss, know that Patty speaks the truth.

Marriage has not diminished Clark's yearning to write. She has recently published *Daddy's Little Girl* (2002), as well as her memoirs, *Kitchen Privileges*, and is currently completing her twentieth novel of suspense, tentatively entitled *The Second Time Around*. Now, however, she has both a competitor and a collaborator rather close to home. Her second daughter, Carol Higgins Clark, has joined her mother on the bestseller lists with her own series of mystery novels featuring serial detective Regan Reilly. Carol, who once typed her mother's manuscripts for her and "took notes," as she says, "on what I thought worked and didn't work" (Siegel), published her first novel, *Decked*, in 1993. Her mother, who believes that Carol "probably honed her skills" as her typist, makes clear that Regan Reilly's creator has her own style and has succeeded on her own talent. "We write in totally different voices," Clark asserts (Siegel). Mother and daughter enjoy sharing plot ideas and discussing their work with each other, so much so that they began collaborating in 2000, when they published their first joint venture, *Deck the Halls*. The tale of Christmas suspense united Mary Higgins Clark's recurrent amateur sleuth, Alvirah Meehan, and her daughter's serial private investigator in a lighthearted holiday caper. They followed its success the next year with a second collaboration, *He Sees You When You're Sleeping: A Novel*. Crime certainly does pay in the Clark family.

In 1974, before the publication of her first successful novel, Clark consulted a fortune teller, who predicted that she would "make a great deal of money and be famous" (Toepfer, "Clean-Cut" 36). Clark has clearly lived to see the fulfillment of that prophecy. But the "Queen of Suspense," who was hailed as the modern Agatha Christie in the 1980s, still has some way to go to match Dame Agatha's record. As Clark told an interviewer following the publication of her fifth novel, "Agatha Christie wrote about a hundred books, so I only have 95 to go" (Hoopes 57). That number has now dwindled to 72—and Clark continues to work at it.

2

Writing to Form: Mary Higgins Clark and the Conventions of Suspense

Without a doubt, Mary Higgins Clark knows how to weave a tale of mystery and suspense. For more than twenty-five years—since the publication in 1975 of her first suspense novel, *Where Are the Children?*, she has been perfecting a formula that keeps readers turning the pages of her tales of plucky heroines who overcome menace and danger by the force of both their wits and their will. Each year fans count on a new Clark novel of suspense, and she never disappoints them. In fact, she has recently begun to write tales of Christmas suspense and has also created a new team of sleuths in her 1996 collection *My Gal Sunday*. While her novels continue to give readers just what they have come to expect, they seem anything but formulaic because Clark manages to invent enough twists of plot and character to make each uniquely compelling. In each as well she quietly continues to explore the forces of disorder in contemporary society and to reassert the stabilizing effect of traditional human values.

When Clark began her writing career, as her failed biographical novel about George Washington makes clear, she had not yet discovered the genre that would suit her talents. In fact, she confesses, "I hadn't the faintest idea that I could write suspense" ("Always a Storyteller" 10). Clark, however, had been educated in the genre by Agatha Christie, Josephine Tey, Mary Roberts Rinehart, and Charlotte Armstrong, some of its masters. Her own reading, in other words, had prepared her to write suspense novels. She had internalized the genre's conventions, or traditional elements, and to become a master at them herself had only to invent plots and create characters that could elicit a disquieting fear in her readers.

Suspense novels, notes Joan Aiken, herself a practitioner of the genre, are "very hard to define" (246). Neither spy thriller nor police procedural, they rely on mystery but are not mysteries. In other words, the solution to a puzzle is not the primary focus of the tale. Suspense writers place their characters in situations that challenge and even threaten them in order to explore their reactions and reveal their nature and to develop thematic issues as well as to evoke a not unpleasant anxiety in the reader.

Clark observes that she writes books that are "neither mystery, nor suspense." Instead, she writes "a *novel* of suspense. I will never win a prize for writing a suspense story," she claims, "because I don't fall into the strict category of suspense" (Personal interview). Readers of the genre, however, know that when they open a Mary Higgins Clark novel they will get what they expect: "Something nasty and frightening," explains Aiken, "is bound to happen" (246).

"Suspense," observes John Cawelti, "is essentially the writer's ability to evoke in us a temporary sense of fear and uncertainty about the fate of a character we care about. It is a special kind of uncertainty that is always pointed towards a possible solution" (17). For Clark, the best sort of suspense arises from the "ordinary": "The only really scary thing that is universal to all of us," she says, "is when you are going about your ordinary life, doing exactly the right thing—not being silly or foolish or reckless— and something goes wrong. Something happens, and suddenly the ordinary becomes extraordinary" (Stasio, "Dressed to Kill" 7). By exploiting the potential for harm that can occur from common circumstances such as meeting an attractive stranger on a holiday cruise, Clark creates the conditions for suspense, which is, she explains, like "an express train or roller coaster. Once on board, you cannot get off until the ride ends" ("Suspense Writing" 11). To achieve suspense, writers of the genre bring to bear all the elements of the novel and work within long-standing conventions that to some extent define the genre. Among the most important elements are plot, character, and setting.

PLOT

The plot, or sequence of events, of virtually every novel of suspense turns on a situation that threatens the protagonist, or central character. The situation need not be a mystery, a hidden secret, or a confusing puzzle that must be exposed or solved. It frequently is, however, because mystery, as Cawelti asserts, "can intensify and complicate a story of triumph over obstacles or of the successful development of love by increasing suspense and uncertainty and adding further interest to the final resolution" (43). Typically, the plot of a Mary Higgins Clark novel is a combination of mystery and suspense, with suspense predominating. Sometimes, in fact, readers know the identity of the criminal as well as his evil plans early in the novel, thereby eliminating or diminishing the element of mystery altogether. In *On the Street Where You Live* (2001), for instance, readers know that Eric Bailey is stalking the novel's heroine, Emily Graham, long before the police make their discovery. That knowledge eliminates the mystery but intensifies the suspense because readers are powerless, of course, to act on it. Consequently, they grow increasingly anxious about Emily, especially as Clark reveals the full extent of Eric's obsession, and then must watch in horror as she naïvely places herself in danger. What begins as mystery thus becomes suspense as the plot's twists and turns move Clark's endangered heroine inexorably to a life-threatening confrontation with a criminal. Those same twists and turns drive readers inexorably to the novel's conclusion, so great is their need for a resolution of their fear.

Clark's skill at inventing new twists of plot is related at least in part to her belief that the source of suspense is the ordinary, from which springs her choice of some unlikely situations and locales for murder. In *Moonlight Becomes You* (1996), for instance, the murder of her former stepmother draws a fashion photographer, Maggie Holloway, into the seemingly placid world of the privileged elderly in Newport, Rhode Island, where nothing is as it seems. Similarly, in *Pretend You Don't See Her* (1997), Lacey Farrell, a rising star on Manhattan's competitive real estate scene, inadvertently witnesses the murder of a client and becomes guardian of a journal that could implicate others in a previous killing, situations that eventually force her into the Federal Witness Protection Program. Dr. Susan Chandler, a clinical psychologist who hosts a popular radio talk show, finds herself in equally dangerous circumstances in *You Belong to Me* (1998) when the subject of one of her daily programs, women who disappear, makes her the target of a serial killer. Each of these plots turns on Clark's introduction of the extraordinary into the ordinary. Nothing about the lives of these women should lead to their victimization. Indeed, the worlds of fashion photography, real estate, and clinical psychology seem hardly the type to endanger competent professional women who are merely going about their daily business. It is just that fact, however, that makes Clark's plots continually surprising and entertaining. Evil, her plots make clear, lurks just beneath the surface of ordinary life. It is not confined to dangerous back alleys, but can instead rear its head on a cruise ship or in a retirement home. Each new situation, each new locale drive home this disturbing reality, and Clark elicits maximum effect from them all.

One other typical element of the suspense novel is romance. Because Clark's narratives of mystery, secrets, and suspense inevitably include a love interest, some define the genre in which she writes as romantic suspense. Clark herself does not. Granted, "there's always," as she admits, "an important, strong man" (O'Neill 64) in her fiction, and that man typically arrives at the novel's climax to assist the heroine in her struggle with the forces of evil. But the love interest, although a requisite element of romantic suspense, is always a subplot in a Clark novel, subordinated to the primary tale of an endangered heroine who must overcome obstacles primarily by herself. As Clark observes, "The love interest is incidental to the plot. The plot doesn't turn on it."

CHARACTER

This emphasis on the heroine's struggle indicates the importance of character to the suspense novel. Unlike the classical mystery or detective novel, which is, according to Kathleen Gregory Klein, "primarily a puzzle or intellectual game where minimal attention is paid to the sufferings of the victim or even the probable fate of the criminal" (4), the suspense novel depends upon fully realized characters for its effect. "The conflict [in suspense] is on an individual, adversarial level," according to Aiken. "The hero/heroine is pitted not against organized crime or international terrorism, but against a personal enemy, a personal problem." Thus, concludes Aiken, "if either hero or hero's enemy is not a flesh-and-blood, fully rounded, recognizable entity, the tension slackens, the credulity drops" (247).

Clark satisfies this convention of the suspense novel by writing about "*very* nice people who are confronted by the forces of evil and who through their own courage and intelligence work their way through to deliverance" ("Suspense Writing" 11). Not only are they nice, but they are also ordinary. Their niceness makes readers like and care about them; their ordinariness makes readers identify with them. These responses raise the novel's suspense level. If, Clark believes, she can bring readers to think, "This could be me. That could be my daughter. This could happen to us" (Stasio, "Dressed to Kill" 7), then she has tapped into the most disquieting source of suspense—the fear that anyone, even the reader, could become a victim. Consequently, her typical heroine is both worthy and believable.

Clark's trademark heroine has changed little since her introduction in 1975's *Where Are the Children?*. Attractive young women in their early thirties, they are generally competent professionals destined for (if they have not already achieved) career success. Intelligent and resourceful, they are capable of negotiating the maze of tangled relationships and complex situations that threaten their lives. Determined and self-confident, they will not be deterred from righting wrongs and exposing truth, even if doing so puts them at risk. Clark's heroines are neither naïve nor foolhardy, nor have their successes made them jaded or complacent. They are, in fact, decent human beings who care about others, and they are the kind of person about whom others, including readers, care. Even the death of a waitress or a shopkeeper troubles them.

One other distinguishing characteristic of Clark's female protagonists is their independence. Few are romantically involved, yet their solitary status does not trouble them. Certainly they are open to the possibility of love in their lives, and during the course of their struggles to disclose the truth, they usually meet men with the potential to enrich their lives, men ideally suited, in fact, because they value the habits of mind and being that these women possess and would not try to change them. Suspense, however, not romance, is Clark's aim, so her heroines are not dependent on these men, a fact that frequently contributes to their dangerous situations and heightens her novels' disquieting tension.

Because they possess the inner resources to live on their own terms, Clark's heroines generally find it unnecessary to confide in men and are sometimes reluctant to do so. In *Moonlight Becomes You*, for instance, Maggie Holloway keeps to herself her discovery of the mysterious gravesite bells that point her to the criminal, so Neil Stephens is almost at a loss to find her when she suspiciously disappears. Similarly, *You Belong to Me*'s Susan Chandler refuses to share information about the death of Regina Clausen with Dr. Donald Richards, a man with the professional ability to assist her investigations. While the men in their lives may be there in the end to help secure their safety, Clark's heroines actively participate in their own rescues. She may be buried alive, but Maggie never stops ringing the bell that alerts others to her location, and a cut and battered Susan manages to slice through what should have been her death shroud. Lacey Farrell's love interest, Tom Lynch, even disappears for the last fifth of *Pretend You Don't See Her*, proof that Clark's heroines are fully capable of meeting life's challenges on their own. In fact, Lacey actually abandons the Witness Protection Program to resolve her own situation when she realizes that government agents have not been able to prevent the criminals from tracking her to her new life.

While the faces that Clark's heroines present to the world radiate strength of character, they conceal an emotional vulnerability that may account for both their compassion and their appeal. Her heroines have suffered disappointment and have known the pain of loss. The death of a parent or parents clouds the childhoods of some, including *Pretend You Don't See Her*'s Lacey Farrell and *Before I Say Good-Bye*'s Nell MacDermott (2000), leaving them with persistent sadness even as adults. Other heroines, such as *You Belong to Me*'s Susan Chandler and *On the Street Where You Live*'s Emily Graham, have been so deeply hurt by betrayal that they fear to trust again. Clark's heroines do not advertise their pain. In fact, they rarely discuss it and seldom even admit it to themselves. But sadness has certainly tinged their lives. The vagaries of human relationships and the unpredictability of life are, they know from experience, the conditions with which everyone must struggle, and that knowledge gives them empathy for those who also suffer.

Clark's heroines are finely drawn portraits of moral values and right behavior. Her criminals, in contrast, embody moral corruption and wickedness. They generally fall into two categories: those who suffer some personal and private psychological torment and those who lust after wealth, power, and position. All are equally ruthless, and neither type earns her sympathy. In fact, Clark confesses that she takes no "emotional satisfaction out of a book in which the villain is so desperately attractive that I find myself rooting for him to beat the system" ("Suspense Writing" 11). While the suspense novel has taken a decided turn toward probing the mind of the criminal and thereby locating the thrill and horror within deviancy, Clark chooses instead to humanize the victims of crime. In the course of her novels, she gives each victim a history that testifies to his or her reality. Sometimes she even discloses their hopes and dreams for the future, as she does, for instance, with Tiffany Smith, the young waitress in *You Belong to Me*. They are never simply nameless and faceless and thus, by implication, worthless. Her criminals, in contrast, even those with psychological problems that may explain but not excuse their cruelty, are never really worthy of sympathy. The killer who calls himself Owen Adams in *You Belong to Me*, for example, may have hated his stepmother for exerting control of his life, but he could have sought help to cope with his anger. Instead, he perverts his intelligence, killing with both deliberation and relish six people and harming several others. Clark reserves her sympathy for crime's innocent victims because their pain and suffering are truly horrific.

SETTING

"The better formulaic artists," according to Cawelti, "devise means of protracting and complicating suspense" (17). Twists and turns of plot are certainly one strategy for withholding from readers the resolution of uncertainty and menace that is characteristic of the suspense novel. An assortment of possible suspects as well as "red herrings," or false clues, also contributes to the suspense novel's edge, and Clark exploits all of these tactics. She also relies on another narrative element, setting, as an "essential [contributor] to a successful suspense novel" ("Suspense Writing" 10).

Clark is adept at using both time and place to heighten the tension of her fiction, frequently investing buildings with appropriate atmosphere and symbolic resonance. The stately Victorian mansions in Spring Lake, New Jersey, for example, are the beautiful façades that conceal the grim realities of sexual predators and grisly death in *On the Street Where You Live*. Similarly, the stark, clinical corridors of modern hospitals, which Clark had used to such effect in novels such as *The Cradle Will Fall* (1980) and *I'll Be Seeing You* (1993), continue to evoke the terror of science gone wrong in 1999's *We'll Meet Again*. Whether her story takes place on a luxurious cruise ship, in a comfortable retirement home, or even in midtown Manhattan, Clark finds just the right details to enhance the atmosphere of foreboding and terror. Ordinariness, moreover, works again to her advantage. Her readers probably have experience of such places, so the "What if" of the plot is thus not only plausible but also personal. They can, in other words, imagine themselves victims of ruthless criminals.

More important than place, however, is time, for as Clark notes, "the containment of time makes for more excitement" (O'Neill 64). Clark confines all of her tales to a limited time frame—a weekend, a week, seldom longer than a month—and from the beginning of the novel, readers know that a dangerous deadline is fast approaching for the heroine. Clark exploits this strategy to great effect in her tales of Christmas suspense, all of which demand that their menace be banished by Christmas morning. She uses the calendar to equal effect in *On the Street Where You Live*. In that work, a serial killer who is recreating the murders of three young women more than a century before has determined to make an unsuspecting Emily Graham his final victim. As the anniversary of that murder looms menacingly nearer with each advancing day, Clark raises the novel's tension level to propel readers toward the climax. Clark remains committed to her view that "the suspense is considerably greater" in a book in which "people are kidnapped and the villain plans to execute them at a specific time" than in a book in which "the reader is only generally concerned about the victims' welfare" ("Suspense Writing" 10). The constraint of time is thus a hallmark of her fiction.

CLARK'S BODY OF WORK

With the 1975 publication of her first successful novel, *Where Are the Children?*, Clark, as Thomas Whissen asserts, "established herself as anything but a mere spinner of suspense novels about distraught heroines menaced by villains and rescued by Mr. Right" (67). Eighteen best-selling novels later, Clark continues to exploit the conventions of mystery and suspense in her own inimitable style. Other writers, particularly Patricia Cornwell and Kathy Reichs, have made serial killers the focus of their forensic investigators, Kay Scarpetta and Tempe Brennan, respectively, providing graphic details of violated bodies and chilling scenes of murder. The new breed of female detectives that includes Sara Paretsky's V. I. Warshawski and Sue Grafton's Kinsey Millhone are as hard-boiled as their traditional male counterparts, able to land a well-placed punch or kick and a fair aim with a revolver. The contemporary female heroines of most mystery-suspense-detective fiction also have lovers, not simply love interests. Clark's fiction, in contrast, is rather tame by contemporary standards. She eschews gruesome depictions of death and generally fades out, like a motion picture shot, on scenes of horrific violence, leaving to her readers' imaginations the grim details. She leaves them as well to fantasize about the heroine's romantic possibilities, for seldom do her attractive young female protagonists bestow even a kiss on the men with whom they share mutual attractions. In many ways, Clark's suspense novels seem a bit of an anachronism in this age of bloody thrillers; her chaste heroines seem as old-fashioned as cotton underwear. Clark finds it amusing, however, that readers and critics refer to her fiction as "clean" and that she is frequently classified as a writer of what the British call the cozy mystery. The subject of her first suspense novel, after all, was child sexual molestation, as it was in her ninth, 1992's *All Around the Town*. Sexual predators, moreover, threaten the women in *Loves Music, Loves to Dance* (1991), *Moonlight Becomes You*, and *On the Street Where You Live*. Clark is not afraid to confront the grim realities of the contemporary world, for as she says, "It's not the subject but the way you treat the subject" (Toepfer, "Clean-Cut" 36).

Clark began her career with a period of experimentation with different types of mystery fiction that included the gothic thriller, in 1982's *A Cry in the Night;* the medical thriller, in 1980's *The Cradle Will Fall;* the political thriller, in 1984's *Stillwatch;* and the celebrity mystery, in 1987's *Weep No More, My Lady.* In the four novels that began with 1989's *While My Pretty One Sleeps,* however, she found the subjects and settings that are truly hers. Set almost exclusively in New York City, these novels, which include *Loves Music, Loves to Dance, All Around the Town,* and *I'll Be Seeing You,* feature "a savvier breed of heroine," according to Whissen (67), a professional woman of wit and intelligence who moves in sophisticated circles. They also have a contemporary edge that mirrors the increasingly complex and cosmopolitan society of late-twentieth-century urban America, a place that seems chaotic and hostile to the uninitiated. These subjects and settings characterize Clark's recent fiction as well.

Moonlight Becomes You, for instance, may be set in Newport, Rhode Island, but its protagonist, fashion photographer Maggie Holloway, is simply visiting the traditional summer retreat of affluent New Yorkers, and *Pretend You Don't See Her's* Lacey Farrell finds herself in Minnesota after being forced to flee a lucrative Manhattan real estate career to save her life. Susan Chandler, the heroine of *You Belong to Me,* is a Manhattan psychologist, and Nell MacDermott is actually elected to represent her Manhattan congressional district at the end of *Before I Say Good-Bye. We'll Meet Again's* Molly Carpenter Lasch, who had a brief but satisfying publishing career in New York City before marriage to a doctor brought her to Greenwich, Connecticut, ends her ordeal prepared to resume her previous life, and Emily Graham, a Chicago native, abandons her past in upstate New York following a painful divorce to join a prestigious Manhattan law firm in *On the Street Where You Live.* A native New Yorker who moves among its privileged society, including its affluent bedroom communities, Clark writes from experience about her fictional world, a fact that lends authenticity to it.

Clark's recent novels also continue to explore contemporary social issues with candor and sensitivity. *You Belong to Me* and *On the Street Where You Live,* for instance, feature sexual predators and serial killers, an acknowledgment of the dangers faced by independent women in a postfeminist world. Moral and ethical issues feature in two other works: *Before I Say Good-Bye* offers an indictment of corruption in the construction industry while *We'll Meet Again* confronts the abuses of health management organizations. Clark understands contemporary disillusionment and alienation. She knows as well the anxiety and fear that the litany of robberies, drive-by shootings, abductions, rapes, and murders broadcast on the nightly news engenders in her readers. She taps into their disquietude when she explores such social issues, making it clear that they affect everyone. Nevertheless, she leaves them with some measure of hope and relief in doing so. Because the novel of suspense, like the mystery, the police procedural, and the thriller, is by convention on the side of law and order, her criminals are punished by the end of her story, and order is restored. The triumph of goodness thus suggests that traditional human values can defeat even the basest human instincts.

Clark earned her reputation as a novelist, but she has also ventured into the realm of the short story, publishing three collections during her career. *The Anastasia Syndrome and Other Stories* (1989), in addition to its title novella, a tale of psychological possession, contains three stories that epitomize Clark's style. The collection's best entry, "Terror Stalks the Class Reunion," is a taut and fast-paced tale of psychopathic obsession that nearly turns disastrous, pure Clark in every way. In *The Lottery Winner: Alvirah and Willy Stories* (1994), Clark resurrects Alvirah Meehan, the former cleaning lady who, in *Weep No More, My Lady*, wins forty million dollars in the lottery and then, indulging a whim, heads for Cypress Point Spa, the book's setting, where she nearly meets her death. In *The Lottery Winner*, the ever-resourceful Alvirah, who has turned amateur sleuth, and her dependable husband, Willy, find themselves escaping danger and solving crimes in stories characterized by gentle humor and subtle wit, qualities that Clark is rarely able to infuse into her novels given their terrifying situations and serious subject matter. Alvirah is clearly a favorite character, and her recurrence not only in these stories but also in two of Clark's tales of Christmas suspense suggests that she functions as the authorial voice as no other character does. Clark's third short story collection, *My Gal Sunday*, which she describes as "suspense with a touch of whimsy," focuses on a charismatic former president, Henry Parker Britland IV, and his congresswoman wife, Sandra "Sunday" O'Brien Britland. The stories, which are as much about the Britland relationship as they are about mystery and suspense, are essentially romances built onto the frame of a "whodunit." Popular successes all, the collections, which are fully discussed in chapter 3, reveal both the strengths and weaknesses of Clark's fiction and suggest that her talents are best suited to the long form.

In 1995, Clark ventured into new territory, publishing the first of four tales of Christmas suspense, *Silent Night*. She followed this poignant tale of faith rewarded with *All Through the Night* (1998), an equally touching tale of hope featuring her amateur sleuths Alvirah and Willy Meehan. Two years later, Clark published the first of two Christmas collaborations with her daughter, the mystery writer Carol Higgins Clark. *Deck the Halls* (2000) and *He Sees You When You're Sleeping: A Novel* (2001) are different in tone from Clark's solo efforts, but they share those works' life-affirming messages of faith, hope, and love that reinforce the meaning of the Christmas story.

The key to many of Clark's works ultimately lies in their titles. In her third novel, *The Cradle Will Fall*, Clark began what would become a trademark with *All Around the Town*—giving her works musical titles. Virtually all of her recent novels share a song title or repeat a song lyric. "All around the town," for example, is a refrain from *The Sidewalks of New York*, and "On the Street Where You Live" is a show-stopping tune from the Lerner and Lowe Broadway musical *My Fair Lady*. The songs from which Clark takes her novels' titles are generally romantic ballads, old standards from bygone eras that crooners such as Jerry Vale, who had a hit singing the lyric "Pretend You Don't See Her," made popular. As such, they serve as ironic counterpoints to her novels' plots and themes. "On the Street Where You Live," for instance, is an exuberant celebration of young love in Lerner and Lowe's musical, but in the Mary Higgins Clark world, the men who walk the street where Emily Graham lives are obsessive stalkers and psychopathic killers. What is innocent adoration in one work is pathological symptom in the other, and the conjunction of the two states of being allows Clark to suggest the fine line between them. Clark's musical titles generally make a mockery of the romantic tunes that they evoke, but that fact, of course, is also part of her deliberate intent in using them. The perversion of the ideals and sentiment that those title songs profess makes clear that the contemporary world has lost something of value since they were popular.

MAJOR THEMES

The development of her body of work demonstrates not only the skill with which Clark handles narrative elements but also the psychological insight that she brings to her major themes and concerns. In her best novels, those themes arise from character as much as, if not more than, from plot. Her heroines, in other words, learn something about themselves or their world from their ordeals, lessons that Clark wishes also to share with her readers. Perhaps the most persistent theme throughout her career has been the interconnections between the past and the present. Sometimes those connections function on a sociological level, as they do in *On the Street Where You Live*, where a series of parallel murders separated by a century allows Clark to draw comparisons about manners and mores in different periods and to challenge the comforting notion of "the good old days." More often, however, those connections are personal. Clark's heroines frequently suffer because they fear the past that haunts them. *We'll Meet Again*'s Molly Carpenter Lasch, for instance, spends nearly six years in prison for a murder she did not commit because she slips into dissociative amnesia and depression following the traumatic discovery of her husband's body and cannot save herself. The continuing presence of the past is a recurrent theme in Clark's novels, and she generally connects it to a second recurrent theme, the nature of selfhood.

Clark's heroines may be self-aware and self-confident, or at least give the appearance of utter self-confidence, but they are still capable of growth. Virtually all of them suffer some private pain—a disappointment, a betrayal, a loss—that clouds their happiness. Although they tend not to dwell on their hurt, giving the impression that they have faced their demons, they have more commonly locked away their doubts, fears, and pain in the dark recesses of their minds and souls. *You Belong to Me*'s Susan Chandler, for example, is reluctant to love again following her sister's betrayal of trust, but equally unwilling to challenge her when she begins to replay that hurtful past, feeling at some level unworthy of love. Similarly, her parents' deaths when she was a young girl have made *Before I Say Good-Bye*'s Nell MacDermott "heart-hungry" (294), a condition she does not admit until after a disastrous marriage. Clark's heroines, however, must eventually release and confront the ghosts of the past. Their recompense for doing so is a new maturity and a deepened sense of self.

Clark relates both of her major themes to a third point that has become increasingly predominant in her recent novels—the complex nature of grief. Young widows such as *We'll Meet Again*'s Molly Carpenter Lasch, *Moonlight Becomes You*'s Maggie Holloway, and *Before I Say Good-Bye*'s Nell MacDermott feature prominently among her recent heroines. Other heroines, including *Pretend You Don't See Her*'s Lacey Farrell, also grieve losses that shake their sense of self. Clark, who was herself a young widow, writes with authority about the pain, the anger, the guilt, the sadness, indeed the whole complex of emotions that accompany a loved one's death. She recognizes that it is in some ways a death of the self and that it requires an honest appraisal of the past before survivors can move forward into the future. Her moving evocation of that process, particularly in the aptly titled *Before I Say Good-Bye*, takes Clark beyond the conventions of most genre fiction.

At the end of a Mary Higgins Clark novel of suspense, readers take satisfaction in the restoration of order and rationality to an otherwise chaotic world where evil invades even the lives of the innocent and the good. That is, after all, one of the conventions of the genre. Clark's endings, however, come not only from the genre's demands but also from her genuine belief in traditional human values. Clark is certainly aware of the forces of disorder in contemporary society. Indeed, she dramatizes them in her fiction. But she, like her heroines, possesses a positive world view and the conviction that right action is a powerful force in life. In novel after novel, she places her ordinary heroines in extraordinary circumstances, and they prevail over evil because they are honest and true, compassionate and caring, and because they refuse to submit to calamity. The restoration of order does not come easy in a Mary Higgins Clark novel, but that it comes is a powerful and comforting endorsement of humanity.

Clark the Storyteller

The short story is a challenge to fiction writers. Like the novel, it exploits the literary elements of plot, character, point of view, setting, tone, and symbol to develop a theme. A compressed form, however, generally no more than three to twenty pages, or short enough to be read in one sitting, the short story demands focus. Its cast of characters must be limited; its plot tightly constructed. In fact, the subplots that are often so important to the novel's development of character and theme must virtually disappear from the short story if it is to sustain its focus and make its point. Expansiveness simply does not suit the form. Nor is every writer capable of mastering it.

Tales of mystery and suspense have generally been well suited to the short story. In fact, Edgar Allan Poe and Sir Arthur Conan Doyle virtually invented the genre in that form. Poe's "The Purloined Letter" and "The Tell-Tale Heart," for example, and Doyle's Sherlock Holmes adventures about "The Speckled Band" and "The Dancing Men," among others, helped to establish the conventions, or standard features, of the mystery and suspense genres and proved the effectiveness of the short story's form for these writers' purposes. Their works still set the standard for contemporary writers of the genres, including Mary Higgins Clark.

In 1989, her reputation firmly established, Clark published the first of three short story collections, *The Anastasia Syndrome and Other Stories*. Five years later, she resurrected a favorite character from her 1987 novel *Weep*

No More, My Lady, Alvirah Meehan, in a series of adventures published as *The Lottery Winner: Alvirah and Willy Stories*. In 1996, a second sleuthing duo, Henry Parker Britland IV and his wife Sandra O'Brien Britland, featured in a collection of four stories entitled *My Gal Sunday*. Popular successes all, the collections reveal both the strengths and the weaknesses of Clark's fiction. A writer of intricate plots, Clark seems at times to chafe against the short story's restriction of length. A creator of believable characters, she seems as well to find the short story's compression a constraint upon their full development. In fact, Clark's best stories are not short, but relatively long, or they are part of a series of connected stories, forming what some critics term a composite novel. In the long story or the serial story, Clark finds the form or technique to overcome some of the limitations inherent in the short story form and to create some satisfying tales of mystery and suspense.

THE ANASTASIA SYNDROME AND OTHER STORIES (1989)

Clark's first story collection is a disparate group of five rather unrelated works. They range from tales of possession spanning three centuries and obsessive love at a class reunion to a case of vengeful murder and a Christmas reunion between mother and child. Their one common link is an element of psychic phenomena. As Clark says of the collection, "The book reflects an intense personal interest on my part in such phenomena as sixth sense and thought transference" ("An Interview"). In the best of the stories, "Terror Stalks the Class Reunion" and "Double Vision," Clark maintains the tense suspense and psychological realism characteristic of her work. The other stories, however, lack one or both of these key ingredients. In the title work, *The Anastasia Syndrome*, a novella rather than a story, character development undermines Clark's intriguing premise. The remaining stories, "Lucky Day" and "The Lost Angel," are too short on suspense to be really gripping. Clark's first story collection is thus her most uneven, perhaps because she has not yet discovered the strategies that will help her to overcome the short story's conventions.

A tale of supernatural suspense that explores the connections between the past and the present, *The Anastasia Syndrome* develops an intriguing premise. Judith Chase, the central character, is a writer whose historical studies have earned acclaim in her dual homelands, the United Kingdom and the United States. Conducting research in London for her current project, a history of the English Civil War, she is also preparing for her marriage to Sir Stephen Hallett, the man expected to become Great Britain's next prime minister. Orphaned during World War II, Judith is also attempting to trace her origins, for she is suffering a type of post-traumatic stress syndrome, reliving the trauma of her separation from her mother during an air raid. In her quest, she visits Dr. Reza Patel, a renowned psychiatrist who has been conducting experiments in regression. During treatment, Judith regresses to the seventeenth century, where the spirit of Lady Margaret Carew possesses her body and soul. Lady Margaret and her family had been victims of the English Civil War, forfeiting their lives and their property to the devious plots of the greedy Simon Hallet. Prior to her execution, Lady Margaret had vowed revenge on her enemy. Judith Chase becomes the unsuspecting vehicle of that revenge.

A short novel, or novella, *The Anastasia Syndrome* has sufficient length for Clark to weave her intricate plot. Nevertheless, she fails to make it convincing because the supernatural elements of the tale do not bear sufficient connection to natural phenomena to be believable. Nor do Judith Chase's actions ring psychologically true. Unlike the concept of multiple personalities, which Clark exploits successfully in 1992's *All Around the Town*, regression to another time and possession by another person from that time are highly improbable to most readers. Some might be willing to suspend disbelief to entertain notions of ghosts and other supernatural phenomena. Yet those same readers would probably find it impossible to believe that an intelligent and assertive modern woman—even if she is suffering from a profound identity crisis and possessed by the spirit of another person—would seduce a construction worker or plant bombs in central London without some recognition of her actions. Judith Chase does both. Clark's farfetched plot device simply cannot sustain the suspension of disbelief on which a successful tale of supernatural suspense depends.

Clark's narrative strategy also undermines *The Anastasia Syndrome*, for it is self-conscious and obtrusive. Italic type marks the shifts from Judith's story to Lady Margaret's story, drawing attention to the movement from present to past and back. Rather than allow the novella's theme to evolve naturally from the interconnections between the plot and the characters of both stories, Clark chooses instead a narrative strategy that forces her point about the relationship between the past and the present. Except for their ancestry and their possession of Edge Barton, the former Carew estate, for instance, Simon Hallet and Sir Stephen Hallett share no common character traits. And although Judith and Lady Margaret are both strong-willed women, Judith lacks the other woman's vindictiveness. Only the manipulations and needs of plot connect the novella's parallel characters.

Thus, Clark's narrative strategy makes it painfully obvious that we are reading two separate stories in this tale.

Like Anna Anderson, the woman who claimed to be the Grand Duchess Anastasia, one of the children of the Russian royal family executed by revolutionaries in 1917, *The Anastasia Syndrome* is compelling but not convincing. It will be five more years, in fact, in 1994's *Remember Me*, before Clark overcomes the technical weaknesses of this novella and effectively weaves together parallel stories. Nevertheless, in *The Anastasia Syndrome* she is clearly pushing the boundaries of her typical literary works.

Much more conventional are the collection's two best pieces, "Terror Stalks the Class Reunion" and "Double Vision." In the first story, Donny Rubel attends his high school reunion to abduct Kay Wesley Crandell, the former teacher for whom he has been nursing a crush since his senior year, eight years before. In the second, Jimmy Cleary, an aspiring actor, determines to murder Caroline Marshall, the woman he holds responsible for his failure, the woman he thought he had killed five years before. Taut and suspenseful, both stories explore extreme psychological states of being. Donny, for instance, is a study in obsession. The class misfit, he has transferred all his longings to belong and to be loved to Kay, the first-year teacher who had befriended him and even asked him to accompany her to the school prom after three girls had refused his invitation. For eight years, Donny has lived a fantasy life with Kay. Now, after stalking her movements with her husband and transforming his appearance, he intends to make Kay his, and he very nearly succeeds. Jimmy Cleary is in his own way as obsessed as Donny, but his obsession is fuelled by vengeance. When Caroline had replaced him in the play she was directing at Rawlings College, she had, so far as he is concerned, handed his big break to Brian Kent. He had tried to make her pay for her act five years before. Instead, he had mistakenly strangled her twin sister Lisa, and Caroline had lived to become a successful attorney. Now, on the eve of her marriage, Jimmy, whose imagined grievances have had plenty of time to fester, has no intention of making another error.

Clark's focus in "Terror Stalks the Class Reunion" and "Double Vision" is clearly the criminal mind. She gets beneath the surface of Donny and Jimmy, probing their motivation and revealing the influences on them—their character flaws, their family backgrounds, their dreams and desires—to make their actions psychologically consistent and thus believable. Donny, for instance, who had never known love, not even from his mother, had grown into an overweight, bespectacled teenager who misinterpreted kindness for the thing he most wanted in life, and Jimmy needed Brian Kent's success to prove his value to his disappointed father. Kay and Caroline, in contrast, typical Clark heroines, strong, intelligent, and resilient, could be interchangeable in the stories. Granted, Clark gives readers sufficient understanding of their characters and lives to render them sympathetic victims, but it is the terrifying glimpse into the deranged mind rather than the desperate struggle against it that makes the greatest impact. Donny and Jimmy are such ordinary monsters that readers shudder to think that everyone has the potential to become like them.

The collection's two other stories, "Lucky Day" and "The Lost Angel," have far less of an edge than any of the others. "Lucky Day," the story of a winning lottery ticket that may have been a motive to murder, begins with an interesting premise, but its resolution in domestic misunderstanding and death by natural causes strips it of its inherent suspense. Its final twist, moreover, is too obvious a plot device to end the story and so makes it seem contrived. In "The Lost Angel," Clark delivers a preview of the tales of Christmas suspense that she will begin to publish with 1995's *Silent Night*. In it, Susan Ahearn, who has searched desperately for the past seven months for the daughter her ex-husband abducted from her, gets a crucial lead on Christmas Eve that takes her from her Midwestern home to New York City. There, she is reunited with her "lost angel," but not before the child has been abandoned at the Port Authority terminal, wandered the streets to Central Park, and then nearly fallen prey to a notorious child molester near Lord and Taylor's. While the story has plenty of plot, too much, really, for its length, it suffers, like "Lucky Day," primarily from a lack of suspense. From the story's opening sentence, it is simply inconceivable that Jamie will fall into the arms of anyone but her mother by its final word. In the end, it seems little more than a preliminary study for more accomplished works to come.

The Anastasia Syndrome and Other Stories certainly contains some good writing, but on balance, it is not Clark at her best. In some stories, she sacrifices too much to plot, leaving character and motivation underdeveloped and subordinating theme to event. In others, she cannot sustain suspense. She even resorts to the obvious and the contrived to control some stories. This disparate group of stories simply does not cohere, so as a whole the collection seems cobbled together from different pieces rather than fashioned by careful design. When Clark next turns her talents to the short story, however, she will have discovered the strategy by which to resolve these problems.

THE LOTTERY WINNER: ALVIRAH AND WILLY STORIES (1994)

In *The Lottery Winner: Alvirah and Willy Stories,* Clark draws on her strengths, especially her realistic characters and intricate plots, to create what is essentially a composite novel, a series of interrelated stories that can stand alone but in conjunction with the others form a unified whole. The common link between these stories is Alvirah and Willy Meehan, the former cleaning lady and plumber whose forty million dollar jackpot in the New York State lottery transforms their lives but not their essential selves. Alvirah and Willy made their first appearance in Clark's fiction in 1987's *Weep No More, My Lady,* where Alvirah, a bit of a busybody who turns her talent to detection, nearly fell victim to a vicious killer—and her own cleverness—at Cypress Point Spa. In fact, in the early drafts of the novel, Clark intended her luck to run out at the exclusive resort. When her daughter Carol protested, however, Clark relented, bringing Alvirah "back from death's door" (Acknowledgments, *The Lottery Winner*) to sleuth again in this short story collection. While each of the stories in *The Lottery Winner* is a mystery complete in itself, Alvirah and Willy's presence in each makes of the works a coherent whole. By using recurrent characters, Clark ensures their full development and hence their believability without having to launch into complete characterizations in each story. She can also emphasize her thematic issues, virtually all of which are embodied in the Meehans. In a hybrid novel form, Clark thus overcomes the weaknesses of her first story collection.

In *The Lottery Winner,* neither time nor money has changed Alvirah Meehan since she nearly met her death at Cypress Point Spa. She still looks upon her world and the people who inhabit it with a mixture of droll humor and innate compassion. She still includes herself among those on whom she focuses her powers of keen observation and insightful evaluation. She still enjoys the challenge of a good mystery—and she still wears the sunburst pin that conceals a miniature tape recorder to assist her investigations. The good life now fits Alvirah like a comfortable shoe. She complains, for instance, of having to fly tourist class in the collection's title story (180). Yet she has never forgotten her humble beginnings, and she is not afraid to return to them. In fact, the old apartment in Flushing where she and Willy had lived prior to their great stroke of luck still awaits their return should fortune demand it (119).

Alvirah is certainly an original. It is simply not in her nature to be anything other than herself. Not many women, for example, would be willing to mangle a Sassoon cut and color by tinting their hair orange-red and hacking it unevenly. Even fewer would be willing to abandon designer clothing and don a cheap purple print outfit. But Alvirah will do both—as well as remove her nail tips—to trap a killer in "Death on the Cape." Alvirah also views her world and herself with the eyes of a realist who cannot be deceived by appearances. In consequence, she injects a comic voice into Clark's tales of mystery and suspense, investing them with a wry humor that is uncharacteristic of her generally sober and somber novels. The humorous tone of the stories in *The Lottery Winner*, however, does nothing to detract from Clark's seriousness of purpose. In their themes and concerns, they are, in fact, utterly characteristic. Yet it is clear that whenever Alvirah Meehan appears, the characteristic takes on new life. Perhaps that explains why Clark allowed her to live to sleuth again.

The collection's title story, "The Lottery Winner," illustrates Clark's continuing regard for her endearing sleuth as well as her continuing preoccupation with the theme of appearance and reality that is central to *Weep No More, My Lady*. In this story, Alvirah returns to Cypress Point Spa to investigate quietly and unofficially the disappearance of the Hayward jewels. Upon her arrival, she quickly develops her list of suspects and begins to penetrate the pleasing surfaces behind which they hide their true selves. In typical Alvirah style, she notes, for instance, that Elyse, Cotter Hayward's ex-wife, "was born with a silver spoon in her mouth." She can also tell "by her voice that Nadine," the current Mrs. Hayward, "isn't a graduate of Miss Porter's" finishing school (189). As always, Alvirah is the person capable of discerning the real thing because she is herself its embodiment.

In an afterword to the collection, Clark observes that "winning the lottery changed the way Alvirah and Willy lived. But it never changed Alvirah and Willy's innate wisdom about what really matters in life"— family, friendship, honesty, good faith, compassion. Every story demonstrates that wealth does not excuse anyone from right behavior and that common human decency makes demands upon us all. As Alvirah muses in "Death on the Cape," "People who don't do the right thing usually don't win in the end" (54). The stories in *The Lottery Winner* provide clear evidence of "the right thing."

The collection's first story, "The Body in the Closet," certainly establishes Clark's thematic concerns. In the story, Alvirah and Willy return from a European holiday to discover the body of the actress Fiona Winters concealed in their bedroom closet. Chief suspect in the murder is Willy's nephew, rising playwright Brian McCormack, who had reason to want

Fiona dead. Not only had she recently ended their romance, but she had also walked out of the lead role in his off-Broadway play, forcing its closure. Brian, who had been staying at the Meehans' Central Park South apartment during their absence and thus had the means to commit the act, would certainly be sitting in prison were it not for the efforts of his aunt. Alvirah, who loves Brian as if he were her own child, is so certain of her nephew's innocence that she investigates alternative suspects when the police ignore evidence that does not fit their theory. Her sleuthing leads to a struggle with the killer on a crumbling thirty-fourth-story balcony from which she is nearly pushed to her death. Nothing, however, not even the threat of death, would ever have deterred Alvirah from protecting her nephew and ensuring his happiness.

Clark dramatizes her themes most forcefully, perhaps, in "Plumbing for Willy." In this story, Alvirah and Willy's television appearance on the Phil Donahue show prompts the kidnapping of the former plumber. Determined to save her husband, Alvirah becomes her old self to solve the case. Dressed in tight jeans, "well-worn sneakers," and a "fleece-lined sweatshirt" (114), remnants from her pre-lottery-winning life, she takes a room service job at the hotel where the kidnappers are holding Willy. Soon, she has discovered his exact location and with some assistance from an unlikely source—a group of nuns—manages to rescue him. Forty million dollars is nothing, after all, without the man she has always loved.

While *The Lottery Winner* may be a collection of stories, it succeeds as a unified work and is in effect a novel. The stories are thematically linked; their tone, or the author's attitude toward the subject, is consistent. Most important, Alvirah Meehan holds them all together, providing a sense of continuity to the various adventures that is missing from Clark's first collection of stories. In *The Lottery Winner*, Clark is again on form because she has discovered the strategies by which to overcome the restrictions of the short story. She will put her discoveries to equally good use in her third collection of short stories, 1996's *My Gal Sunday*.

MY GAL SUNDAY (1996)

Like *The Lottery Winner*, *My Gal Sunday* is essentially a novel written as stories, four rather long stories, to be exact. Ranging from eight to thirty pages, the length of these stories, in fact, confirms one of the requirements of a successful Clark story. Here, Clark devotes every word to the adventures of a new sleuthing duo, the Britlands. Inspired, as she reveals in the collection's Acknowledgments, by her favorite 1940s radio serial, "Our

Gal Sunday," she creates a new husband-and-wife detective team who provide the answer to that program's weekly premise about the attraction of opposites. Henry Parker Britland IV is a dashing former president who, in his mid-forties, is enjoying an early retirement. Sandra O'Brien Britland, his "Sunday," is the young congresswoman who met the country's most eligible bachelor on his final day in the White House and married him six weeks later. Henry is wealthy and worldly, a man who reads six Sunday newspapers in three different languages and who takes personal telephone calls from the queen of England. Sunday, in contrast, the daughter of a motorman on the New Jersey Central Railroad and twelve years her husband's junior, had worked her way through college as well as law school and then won a surprising election victory against a tough incumbent after spending seven years as a public defender. Together they make a formidable team, their differences in background overcome by their love for each other.

The stories in *My Gal Sunday* are as much about the Britland relationship as they are about mystery and suspense. In fact, they are essentially romances built onto the frame of a "whodunit" that provides an opportunity for Henry and Sunday to collaborate. Working together, they demonstrate the qualities that form the basis of true love. Certainly they care for and are concerned about each other, and they share absolute trust in each other as well. Most important, Henry and Sunday respect each other, and thus they allow each other the freedom to be an independent person. Sunday, for instance, admits in the collection's first story, "A Crime of Passion," that she "didn't always agree" with her husband when he served his country (4), and in the third story, "Hail, *Columbia!*," she and Henry engage in a brief political debate about foreign policy (138). Such differences of opinion, however, do not prevent them from admiring each other's commitment to personal beliefs and respecting each other's talents. Henry, in fact, is quick to remind a friend and former colleague who stands accused of murder in "A Crime of Passion" that Sunday is not only an excellent cook but also a skilled defense attorney (15). As Henry and Sunday turn their talents to detection in *My Gal Sunday,* it grows clear that the mystery of love is Clark's real subject here.

As its title suggests, the collection's first story, "A Crime of Passion," clearly focuses on Clark's subject. In it, the newly wed Britlands work to clear Thomas Acker Shipman, Henry's former secretary of state, of the murder of Arabella Young, the shapely beauty half his age with whom he had had a relationship following the death of his beloved wife of nearly thirty years. In the story, Clark sets against each other several different examples of love, from the enduring and the endearing to the trivial and the selfish, to clarify its true shape and form. Shipman's infatuation with Arabella, for instance, which had made him look foolish and caused him to lose his "steely control" (4), was certainly a pale imitation of the deeply satisfying love for Constance that he still warmly remembers (11). It pales as well against the promise of love rekindled with his college sweetheart, the Countess Condazzi, a widow with the maturity to know that Shipman must grieve his loss before he can truly love another (30). As Henry and Sunday sift the evidence and interview suspects, the newlyweds, who are already "on the same wavelength" (2), get a series of lessons on love, but it is also clear that they need none. They recognize the real thing—Shipman's devotion to Constance, Betsy Condazzi's trust in Shipman—because they already know it, and that knowledge will finally help them to recognize a motive for murder.

The Britlands' love is tested in the collection's second, and longest, story, "They All Ran After the President's Wife," when Sunday falls victim to a ruthless kidnapper demanding the release from prison of an international terrorist. A frantic Henry rushes to the White House, where he enlists the aid of the man who now leads the country, his former vice president, but the curious elements of the case stymie all the nation's resources and make it only a matter of time until Sunday meets her death. "They All Ran After the President's Wife" is vintage Clark, featuring an intricate plot and gripping suspense as well as an ending that sets the world to right. It also features a sly bit of humor in its self-obsessed terrorist who cares more about designer labels, vintage wines, and beluga caviar than political goals and causes. The story's true revelation, however, is the depth of Henry's love for Sunday. An expert pilot, he intends to fly the plane that will transport the terrorist from the country and has issued orders that the military should blow it to bits with both of them on it should the kidnapper fail to release Sunday unharmed (81). "Ah, the power of love!" the terrorist sneers, and indeed, that is Clark's point. Without Sunday, "everything would be meaningless" (72) to Henry.

In "Hail, *Columbia!*," the collection's tightly-plotted third story, the Britlands engage in some very traditional sleuthing to solve the decades-old disappearance of Costa Barria's Prime Minister Garcia del Rio aboard the family yacht when Henry was twelve years old. In the tender final story, "Merry Christmas/*Joyeux Noël*," the Britlands become foster parents to a young boy who cannot or will not communicate with those, including Henry and Sunday, who are trying desperately to reunite him with his family by Christmas day. Both stories add to Clark's investigations into true love as well. Despite the political overtones of Prime Minister del Rio's murder, marital betrayal lies at the core of "Hail, *Columbia!*." Angelica del Rio had extorted money from her country, deceived her husband, whom she had only recently married, and plotted his murder in order to seize power for herself. Her actions, of course, make a mockery of her marriage vows and stand in stark contrast to the solidarity and support that the Birtlands, another newlywed couple, so clearly enjoy. In "Merry Christmas/*Joyeux Noël*," their love ripened into fullness, Henry, who has secretly obtained his wife's traditional Christmas ornaments, and Sunday begin to create their own holiday traditions and, with the help of a lost boy, to imagine their home filled with their own children. At the Christmas season, their love strengthened by the adversity of the previous year, they are grateful for their blessings, among which they count each other. "Merry Christmas/*Joyeux Noël*" thus gives fitting closure to Clark's tales of love and mystery.

In 1996, after many years of widowhood, Mary Higgins Clark married John Conheeney, to whom she dedicated *My Gal Sunday.* Her own marital happiness, as well as her firm belief in marital love, certainly seems to be reflected in this collection. Clark, of course, had already provided such evidence in Alvirah and Willy Meehan, who, after forty years of marriage, are as much, if not more, in love with each other as they were on their wedding day. Their mutual devotion had even been important to several stories, especially "Plumbing for Willy," in *The Lottery Winner.* Never before, however, had she thematically subordinated other issues to an exploration of love, as she does in *My Gal Sunday.* Nor had her plots been as much about love and marriage as about mystery and detection as they are in this collection.

My Gal Sunday is ultimately a pleasing indulgence for Clark. The collection's stories are sophisticated fairy tales in which the Britlands embody the romance of power, glamour, and wealth, but deservedly so. After all, people as gracious and charming, as compassionate and loving as Henry and Sunday could never merit anything but approval. The stories' light tone, gentle humor, and subdued menace make their "happily-ever-after" endings inevitable, but certainly not disappointing. Romance has generally been the unexplored territory in Clark's fiction, but in *My Gal Sunday*, she does more than skirt its borders. The result is a map of love.

On balance, Clark's story collections are qualified successes. Certainly they contain some vintage tales that compare favorably to her novels for their imaginative and suspenseful plots, their driving pace, and their psychological insight and thus stand on their own merit. Yet they also include stories that fail to ring true, usually because some literary element is underdeveloped. Within the context of unified and coherent collections such as *The Lottery Winner* and *My Gal Sunday*, however, even weak stories have an impact, for the collections' recurrent characters and consistent themes provide the subtext that makes such stories part of the whole and masks their individual deficiencies. What all of these collections finally demonstrate is that Mary Higgins Clark is at her best in the long form. She succeeds with the short story when it is essentially an episode in a composite novel.

Christmas Suspense

Mystery and suspense are not generally invited to Christmas celebrations. In fact, murder and mayhem are expected to take a holiday during this season of peace, joy, and love. In 1995, however, Mary Higgins Clark opened the door to these uninvited guests, writing the first of a series of short novels set during the Christmas season. *Silent Night*, a poignant tale of faith rewarded, was followed in 1998 by *All Through the Night: A Suspense Story*, a touching story of hope featuring Clark's recurrent characters Alvirah and Willy Meehan. Two years later, Clark published the first of two Christmas collaborations with her daughter, the mystery writer Carol Higgins Clark: *Deck the Halls* (2000), a heartwarming tale of faith and courage, followed by their second joint effort, the touching fantasy *He Sees You When You're Sleeping: A Novel*, in 2001. While the four novels feature variations in plot and especially in tone, or the author's attitude toward the subject, they have in common—in addition to their musical titles—life-affirming messages of faith, hope, and love that reinforce the significance of the Christmas story and are perfectly attuned to the spirit of the season. They are in their own way Clark's Christmas gifts to her readers.

Mary Higgins Clark's tales of Christmas suspense essentially break into two types, the difference between them signified in their titles. Written by Clark on her own, *Silent Night* and *All Through the Night* strike rather solemn notes of peace and love, just like the carols with which they share their titles, and constitute the first type of tale. The menace lurking at their heart is real and significant, posing a dangerous threat to the characters. Even the presence of the rather comic Alvirah Meehan in the second work cannot diminish Clark's serious tone nor her genuine concern for her characters' fates. To capture the spritely rythyms of "Deck the Halls" and "Santa Claus is Coming to Town," the songs from which her second type of tale take their titles, Clark, writing collaboratively with Carol Higgins Clark, strikes a humorous chord, creating a different effect. Despite the dangers that they face, the characters in these works never seem truly threatened because the criminals are laughably inept. Clark's lighthearted tone thus undermines her novels' suspense, making *Deck the Halls* and *He Sees You When You're Sleeping* rather atypical of her work. While the shift in tone is no doubt to some extent the result of her collaboration with her daughter, whose novels have a rather light touch, it also gives evidence of Clark's continuing inclination, first revealed in 1987's *Weep No More, My Lady* with Alvirah's introduction, to indulge her own sense of humor. The holiday season, perhaps, gives her no better time to do so.

SILENT NIGHT (1995)

Clark's first venture into Christmas suspense is the tightly plotted *Silent Night*. In fewer than twenty-four hours, the circumstances surrounding a young boy's abduction by an escaped killer restore the faith of two troubled women, Catherine Dornan and Cally Hunter. Catherine, the thirty-four-year-old wife of Dr. Thomas Dornan, a pediatrician from Omaha, Nebraska, has come to New York City with their two sons, ten-year-old Michael and seven-year-old Brian, to seek treatment at Sloan-Kettering hospital for the leukemia that threatens her husband's life. Grief and despair are etched on her face. But on their way to visit Thomas on Christmas Eve, Catherine takes her sons to view the window displays at Saks Fifth Avenue and the towering tree at Rockefeller Center, hoping to infuse some holiday spirit into the grim reality that they are living.

Hoping to purchase a doll from a street vendor for her four-year-old daughter, Gigi, with the meager eight dollars saved from her paycheck, Cally also finds herself in mid-town Manhattan on Christmas Eve. There, as carolers sing "Silent Night," a bulky wallet falls from the handbag of a woman who looks, to the thirty-year-old nurse's aide at St. Luke's-Roosevelt hospital, as if she has not "a care in the world" (22). A desperate Cally retrieves it and retreats quickly to her shabby apartment, her own grim reality. What neither woman notices is that the only witness to the incident, young Brian Dornan, has given chase. Inside the wallet is the St.

Christopher medal that had saved his grandfather's life during World War II and that he believes will now save his father's life. Brian's desperate quest to retrieve the medal links the lives of these two strangers who share nothing but a vision of a bleak future and brings faith and hope to each on Christmas morning.

On the surface, Clark's two central characters could not be more different, but just beneath it, both Catherine Dornan and Cally Hunter are struggling with issues of doubt and faith. Catherine, a beloved child and wife, has lived a "happily complacent life [that] she had assumed would be hers forever" (24). Hardship has never been her lot; despair and desperation have never tested her spirit. She can thus afford a healthy dose of skepticism about the power of St. Christopher, the patron of travellers. After all, she reminds Brian, Christopher was "only a myth" and is no longer considered a saint by the Roman Catholic church (20). She faces her husband's sickness and Brian's abduction, which occurs after chasing Cally, with quiet dignity and resolve, but fear undermines her faith. Even Thomas, his doctor tells her, senses that she doubts her husband's chances of recovery and urges her to believe, for his sake (41), so Catherine gamely acts a faith she does not feel.

Cally, in contrast, has learned from experience to expect the worst from life. "One of the hard-luck people of this world" (99), she and her younger brother, Jimmy Siddons, had been abandoned by their mother to the care of an elderly grandmother whose death left Cally to try, unsuccessfully, to keep her brother from a life of crime when she was little more than a child herself (99). She and her husband, Frank, had celebrated only one Christmas together, savoring the news that she was pregnant, before a hit-and-run driver made her a widow. Three years later, Gigi was in foster care, and Cally was serving a fifteen-month sentence at the Bedford correctional facility for women for aiding a fugitive—her brother. She had naïvely believed his story about trying to escape from a retaliatory gang fight when she gave him money and her car keys, never suspecting that he had wounded a clerk during a liquor store robbery or anticipating that he would kill the policeman who stopped him for a traffic violation. Recently released from prison and eager to celebrate Christmas, however pinched the circumstances, with Gigi, Cally wants to believe that her life can change, but she has little to give her hope. In fact, she dreads the thought that her brother will reappear in her life, and her face bears the "haunted expression" of a woman who fears the "horror" that she might one day be imprisoned again (99).

Faith, the central theme of *Silent Night*, comes for Catherine and Cally from an unlikely source—a seven-year-old boy. When Brian gives chase to the young woman who has collected his mother's wallet, he cares only to retrieve the St. Christopher medal that he knows will save his father's life. After all, on a Christmas Eve more than fifty years before, it had deflected a bullet that should have killed his Grandpa Cavanaugh during the Battle of the Bulge (119). "Impatient" with his mother's skepticism about the medal (20) and fearful for his father's recovery without its protection, Brian acts on his faith when he follows Cally, and that faith gives him strength when Jimmy Siddons, who has escaped from Riker's Island prison, abducts him from Cally's apartment and holds him hostage as he makes his way north to the Canadian border. Despite his failed attempt to escape from Jimmy's car, Brian experiences a "sense of relief" as he clutches the medal in his hand, and he envisions himself being carried to safety on the shoulders of the saint just as Christopher had once carried the small child across the dangerous river (105). No matter how his faith is tested, Brian never doubts that he will be saved, and eventually his Christopher—Trooper Chris McNally—is there to rescue him when a maniacal Jimmy tries to steer his racing car into the young boy who had dived from the front seat to escape the bullets intended to kill him (146–48). Faith such as Brian's, *Silent Night* makes clear, is always rewarded.

On a silent night centuries before, according to the biblical story, a Christmas Eve much like the one on which Clark has significantly set her novel, the fate of the world hung in the balance. On this silent night, the fate of a young boy and an ailing doctor and the faith of two desperate women, the biblical story's human parallel, are similarly at risk. And just as the events of the first Christmas Eve brought peace and joy and hope to those who believed, so, too, do the events of this one. As Catherine keeps vigil for both her husband and her son, she resists the anger and frustration that have nurtured her skepticism and rediscovers the deep resources of belief. "Faith," she thinks, "—even in something as unlikely as a St. Christopher medal—was a good thing" (77), and that recognition gives her the conviction of her reassuring "Yes, I do" when Michael asks if she truly believes that St. Christopher will save his father and brother (96).

Similarly, Cally must wrestle with her own doubts and fears on this silent night. Distrustful of Jack Shore, the cynical detective whose open hostility and bullying tactics have convinced her that she will never get a fair hearing when police learn that she has once again been coerced into helping her brother, Cally is fearful of informing authorities about Jimmy's abduction of Brian. She simply cannot face further imprisonment and another separation from her daughter, and she does, after all, have Catherine Dornan's wallet. Jimmy, moreover, had threatened to kill his young hostage should she sound the alarm. But Cally, an essentially good woman victimized by the same forces that have threatened Catherine's happy life, cannot in all conscience resist the appeal in Brian's pleading eyes and trembling voice as Jimmy pulled him from her apartment (53). Ignoring her own self-interest and her very real fears about the consequences of her actions, she telephones Mort Levy with information that will save Brian's life, trusting this detective's human approach to policing, and her faith, too, is rewarded. Early Christmas morning, when Levy and his chief, Bud Folney, knock on her door laden with toys and games for her daughter and assurances that she will not face charges for her actions, Cally can only stare in disbelief at these "two beaming, self-appointed Santa Clauses" (151). But she drifts off to sleep secure in her faith that "everything will get better" (151).

Near the end of *Silent Night,* Barbara Cavanaugh, Catherine's mother, tells her grandson Michael the tale of his grandfather's escape from death during World War II. That escape was indeed miraculous, but it occurred only after Grandpa had entered a village church on Christmas Eve, drawn by a chorus of voices singing "Silent Night." Surrounded by fierce fighting and nearly without food, the villagers would not be deterred from attending Midnight Mass, from demonstrating their belief in their survival, and their "faith and courage" helped a frightened twenty-two-year-old soldier to find his own (119). This tale-within-a-tale is a fourth "verse" in Clark's literary Christmas carol; its lyric reinforces the verses devoted to Catherine, Cally, and Brian and reiterates Clark's central theme, the words with which she ends her story, *"All is calm . . . all is bright"* (154). *Silent Night,* like the carol with which the novel shares its title, is Clark's promise of peace and her message of hope.

ALL THROUGH THE NIGHT: A SUSPENSE STORY (1998)

That message of faith and hope is equally central to Clark's second tale of Christmas suspense, *All Through the Night.* A more expansive tale than her first in terms of both plot and character, it spans a period of seven years, although its principal action occurs during one crucial three week, pre-Christmas period, and resurrects Clark's amateur sleuth Alvirah Meehan. Its various plot threads, however, and numerous characters are all connected to the novel's chief concern—the fate of a child, and, by extension, the well-being of all children. So like the carol from which the novel takes its title, *All Through the Night* is a lullaby offering the reassurance of protection from harm. In it, Clark delivers a human host of guardian angels determined to protect one small girl and to shelter a neighborhood's latch-key children, creating a parallel version of the Biblical Christmas story.

Clark establishes her primary plot thread in the prologue to *All Through the Night*, dramatizing a series of key events that occur seven years before her novel's contemporary action. On a cold December evening twenty-two days before Christmas, a desperate nineteen-year-old, Sondra Lewis, abandons her newborn daughter on the steps of St. Clement's church and then places an anonymous telephone call to the rectory to ensure that Monsignor Ferris finds the baby and secures a good home for her. Sondra's intentions, however, go all wrong, for inside St. Clement's, Lenny Centino has just robbed the church's offering boxes and stolen its one treasure, a silver and diamond chalice, but not before a silent alarm has alerted police to the theft. To cover his escape, Lenny shoves his backpack into the foot of an unattended stroller on the church steps that appears to hold nothing but shopping bags and walks sedately down the pavement, the perfect image of a loving father, which he has just inadvertently become. Inside that stroller lies Sondra's sleeping daughter. By the time he hears the infant's crying, Lenny has already reached the safety of his aunt's apartment, where he claims the child as his own, names her Star, and gives her to the care of his seventy-four-year-old aunt, Lilly Maldonado. Meanwhile, Sondra boards the bus that takes her to Birmingham, Alabama, where she studies the violin, convinced that her child is in the care of Monsignor Ferris because Father Dailey, who had answered her telephone call, had told her that the Monsignor was attending to a police emergency. It will be seven years before she learns the truth about the nature of that emergency and the events of that December night.

When the novel's contemporary action begins, the events it dramatizes seem unrelated to those that occurred exactly seven years before. Three weeks before Christmas, Alvirah and Willy Meehan are preparing to attend the funeral of Bessie Durkin Maher, a crusty, eighty-eight-year-old who had had a "lifelong habit of getting other people," especially her seventy-five-year-old sister Kate Durkin, "to do things her way" (28). At Bessie's death, Kate expects to inherit her sister's New York townhouse and announces her intention on the day of the funeral to donate it to Home Base, an unofficial after-school center for young children run by Sister Cordelia, Willy's eldest sibling. Threatened by the city with closure at the new year, Home Base itself needs a home where it will be able to continue to provide shelter for some of New York's most endangered citizens, children who would have only an empty apartment or the streets to which to return at the end of the school day. Kate's generosity gives comfort to all at Bessie's funeral except the tenants of the townhouse's top floor apartment, Vic and Linda Baker. When the Bakers, however, produce a new will giving them ownership of the house and effectively dispossessing Home Base and evicting Kate, who will move rather than become a tenant in her own home, disbelief and distress follow relief. Convinced that Bessie, although decidedly "house proud" (61), would never have contradicted her stated intentions in this way or treated her sister so shabbily, Alvirah determines to break the new will, and so begins what she call "The case of Bessie's will" (70). Soon, as they usually do, Alvirah's investigations have spiraled into other mysteries, and the amateur sleuth is pursuing as well the case of the unhappy woman of St. Clement's church and solving in the process the case of the missing chalice. For each is connected to the events of the novel's prologue and the fate of one innocent child, and thus the threads of Clark's plot form their pattern and design.

Clark admits in the Acknowledgments to *All Through the Night* that the prospect of resurrecting Alvirah and Willy lured her into writing her second tale of Christmas suspense, and her genuine affection for them enlivens their characterization. The former cleaning woman and plumber who had won a forty-million-dollar lottery jackpot made their debut appearance in 1987's *Weep No More, My Lady* and were then the focus of a collection of short stories, *The Lottery Winner* (1994). Money may have given them an apartment overlooking Central Park, smart new wardrobes, and an illustrious circle of friends and acquaintances, but their essential generosity and compassion have remained constant through the years. In fact, they have never forgotten how to live without money and value above all their mutual love and devotion (21–22). Sensitive to others' needs but utterly pragmatic about life, Alvirah never minces words, nor does she shrink from a problem. In *All Through the Night*, she is in rare form, particularly when she takes on the Bakers, slick con artists who, she discovers, prey on elderly property owners. Her verbal barbs at them never miss their target. She is equally fine when she refuses to judge harshly a repentant Sondra Lewis for abandoning her baby and determines instead to reunite mother and child. Alvirah Meehan, the self-described "lottery winner, problem solver and contributing columnist to the *New York Globe*" (116), is without doubt the authorial voice of this novel, expressing Clark's own attitudes and beliefs. Clark likes her, so readers like her. Through

Alvirah, she thus controls their understanding of the novel's various elements.

Alvirah's sympathetic understanding of the circumstances that prompted Sondra Lewis to abandon her newborn daughter is particularly crucial to Clark's characterization of this troubled young woman. Whereas some might find her guilty of criminal neglect, Alvirah, and through her, Clark's readers, sees instead a sacrificial act of love. Raised in Chicago by her elderly grandfather following her parents' deaths, Sondra was a lonely violin student at the University of Alabama when, seduced by the attentions of a visiting pianist, she found herself pregnant following their brief affair. Fearful of disappointing her grandfather, who had dedicated his life to nurturing her talent and thus ensuring that she would have the musical career that crippling arthritis had denied him, Sondra can see only one course of action to her situation. That course of action brings her to St. Clement's church on a cold December evening and draws her back daily when, on the verge of professional success, she next returns to New York.

Alvirah certainly does not condone Sondra's act, but she does accept her genuine repentance for it. Sondra, after all, does not want to reclaim her daughter from the happy, loving home in which she has imagined her thriving all these years. She simply wants reassurance that such a life has indeed been her child's. She does not expect more from life because her judgment of herself is harsh: "I traded my baby," she thinks, "for my grandfather's good opinion of me and my own chance of success" (44). Now, she takes no joy in her impending debut at Carnegie Hall, and indeed, she even withholds herself from her music. As her grandfather chides her, she may have perfected her technical virtuosity, but she fails utterly to convey her music's emotional intensity (170). Half of Sondra Lewis, as Alvirah instinctively recognizes, went missing on the day that she abandoned her daughter. Alvirah wants now to make her whole and bring her peace. She has earned that release from guilt.

At the center of all three of Alvirah's cases is the child known as Stellina Centino, *All Through the Night*'s "little star." A "grave and oddly composed" (56) child with sad eyes and a beautiful singing voice, Stellina is certainly no carefree seven-year-old. The woman she knows as her Nonna, or grandmother, and who has raised her from infancy, Lenny's aunt Lilly Maldonado, grows increasingly weak each day, and Stellina worries about her. She dreads, too, those unexpected visits from the man she knows as her father because she feels frightened when he takes her to places where he argues with the people who give him money and because he argues with Nonna, too (64). She wants most the impossible—her mother's return—so keeps as a "talisman" (95) a silver chalice that she believes had been hers. Twining her fingers about its smooth surface, Stellina can "feel her mother's hands still holding it" (96). Her faith, she believes, will someday bring her mother to her.

Clark invests Stellina with symbolic significance, and thus she carries the weight of *All Through the Night*'s central themes. Her name, for instance, evokes a heavenly body, a guiding star of faith and hope, which she is both in herself and for others, but especially for her mother, Sondra Lewis. Stellina never breaks faith that her prayer will be answered, and, of course, it eventually is. Her chalice—St. Clement's stolen treasure—provides crucial evidence of her true identity and leads to her reunion with her mother, thereby demonstrating, as Alvirah says, that "if you believe hard enough and long enough, your wishes can come true" (201), one of the novel's major themes. That reunion also resurrects the spirit of a young woman who, believing that she deserved none, could find no joy in life. Having found her other half, however, Sondra can bring heartfelt intensity to her music because her little star shines bright in the audience. Bishop Santori's chalice has certainly fulfilled in its "exile" the "greater mission" that Monsignor Ferris had frequently imagined for it (128).

As one of the children who attend Home Base after-school programs, Stellina also embodies the novel's theme of shelter on both a personal and a representative level. Dressed in her blue and white robes for her role as the Virgin Mary in the Home Base Christmas pageant, Stellina enacts the biblical story of a child born in a stable because there was no room for him at the inn, no other shelter for him from the cold. In the threatened closure of Home Base, Clark develops the implications of that situation. Stellina and her fellow actors will be put at risk should Home Base fail to find a home. They will be without a place of shelter in which to thrive, their present blighted, their future bleak. Lilly Maldonado's serious illness puts Stellina even further at risk because Lenny intends to seize this opportunity to reclaim the girl and use her again as cover for his drug deliveries. Children, Clark's novel makes clear, need and deserve shelter, protection from the harsh realities of life, the people and situations that endanger their well-being, and a society that cannot provide it fails in its duty. In the fate of a child lies the fate of us all: That was the message of the Biblical Christmas story. It is the primary message of *All Through the Night* as well.

DECK THE HALLS (2000)

Clark's third tale of Christmas suspense, *Deck the Halls,* takes a decidedly different tone from her previous efforts. Written with coauthor Carol Higgins Clark, the novel unites each writer's recurrent sleuths, the lottery winner Alvirah Meehan and the private investigator Regan Reilly, in a case of kidnap and ransom that threatens to destroy the Christmas season for its two undeserving subjects and their families. Mother and daughter clearly enjoyed their collaboration, for their tale has a decidedly mischievous, tongue-in-cheek humor that especially enlivens the characterization of its inept villains. That humor, however, diminishes the sense of genuine menace that is typically Clark's, so the novel's suspense, despite plot complications that include a bungled ransom attempt and a winter blizzard, is rather flat. Readers are never in any doubt about the kidnapping's outcome—but perhaps that is as it should be in a Christmas tale of faith and hope.

Deck the Halls finds Nora Regan Reilly, a popular mystery writer with a distinct resemblance to Mary Higgins Clark herself, in a Manhattan hospital three days before Christmas following surgery to set a broken leg. At her side are her daughter, Regan Reilly, a thirty-one-year-old private investigator who has just arrived on the red-eye flight from her Los Angeles home (and who bears a decided resemblance to her creator, Carol Higgins Clark), and Nora's husband, Luke Reilly, the owner of three funeral homes, dubbed "Reilly's Remains" (34) by his loving wife and daughter. Their plans for a Hawaiian holiday dashed, Regan sets about alternate Christmas preparations while Luke goes off to a dental appointment and the funeral of the eccentric millionaire Cuthbert Boniface Goodloe. He keeps neither engagement, however, because Goodloe's disgruntled nephew, Cuthbert Boniface "C. B." Dingle, and his hapless accomplice, Petey "the Painter" Commet, abduct Luke and his employee, Rosita Gonzalez, and hold them for a one-million-dollar-ransom on a dilapidated houseboat anchored precariously in the Hudson River.

Concerned by her father's uncharacteristic behavior, Regan goes to his dentist's in search of him. There she meets Alvirah Meehan, a fan of her mother's crime novels, who has accompanied Willy for treatment. When the ransom call alerts Regan to her father's situation, a sympathetic Alvirah, who is, as her husband says, "always at full throttle, looking for trouble" (45), offers her assistance. Before long, the private investigator and the "roving crime correspondent" (45) are tracking two inept kidnappers whose very inexperience compounds their dangerousness. Only when Alvirah realizes that the kidnappers are recreating a Nora Regan Reilly mystery plot do they get the break that leads to Luke's and Rosita's rescue and holiday reunions with their loved ones.

Unlike Clark's previous tales of Christmas suspense, *Deck the Halls* is plot-driven rather than character-driven. In other words, the sequence of events rather than the development of character moves the tale to its conclusion. In *Silent Night*, Clark created two complex characters experiencing crises of faith, and in *All Through the Night*, she focused on a guilt-stricken young woman who must come to forgive herself. No such crises of self, however, provide depth to *Deck the Halls*'s cast of characters. Certainly the Clarks provide them with pertinent facts and background details. Readers learn, for instance, that Rosita, the mother of two young boys, has been deserted by her husband and that Fred Torres, the twenty-eight-year-old policeman who forgoes his Caribbean holiday to care for her sons, is studying for his law degree. Such information establishes the reality of her central characters, but the novel's action never really alters that reality. The Reillys, the Meehans, Rosita, and Fred are the same upright characters at the end of their experience as they are at the beginning. The kidnapping has done nothing more than increase their love of each other and their appreciation for their good fortune.

Equally static is the tale's cast of secondary characters, but here, at least, the Clarks have enlivened their depiction with humor and wit. The aptly named Ernest Bumbles, for instance, president and chairman of the board of the Seed-Plant-Bloom-and-Blossom Society of the Garden State of New Jersey, the surprise beneficiary of Goodloe's will, provides a good measure of comic relief to *Deck the Halls* by his innocent pursuit of Luke Reilly. So pleased is he with the framed proclamation expressing the Blossoms' effusive gratitude for Reilly's role in their recent good fortune that he determines to present it to him before leaving town on Christmas Eve. He thus appears or telephones at auspicious times, earnestly bumbling into Luke's ordeal because he knows nothing of it. Similarly, Alvin Luck, the unlucky author of twelve unpublished suspense novels, becomes an equally unlucky kidnap suspect when he sends a gift to his favorite mystery writer, Nora Regan Reilly, that suggests knowledge of the crime. It is *Deck the Halls*'s kidnappers, however, who deliver most of its humor.

The hapless Petey the Painter, for instance, takes childish pleasure in the game he is playing, more concerned about the stale bread on his ham and cheese sandwich (88) than the consequences of his act because the possibility of failure has never crossed his mind. For this reason, too, and because he is incapable of silence, he keeps up a running banter of conversation that discloses far too much information to his captives, including his and C. B.'s intent to live out their lives in luxury on a Brazilian beach with the ransom money. This Commet's brilliance is certainly far from celestial.

C. B. Dingle, for his part, is only a little less dense than his partner-in-crime. For years he has endured bearing his uncle's name, believing it will ensure his inheritance. When his uncle, however, bequeaths the bulk of his estate to Ernest Bumble's Blossoms, a bitter C. B. determines to secure his fortune from the man he holds responsible for his situation, Luke Reilly. It was Reilly, after all, who had introduced his uncle to the Blossoms. From the moment C. B. makes Petey his accomplice, however, he has foiled his own plan, and by the time the police apprehend him, he has realized that "maybe jail was preferable to a lifetime in Brazil with Petey" (200).

Deck the Halls's kidnappers are certainly colorful characters who prompt chuckles from its readers. Those chuckles, however, diminish the kidnappers' menace and undermine the plot's seriousness. It is impossible to fear villains who squabble about meals (38; 92), call each other "moron" and "Mr. Hoity-toity" (112), and actually leave their prisoners unguarded to go one last time (and because they do not want to miss the holiday snacks) to happy hour at Elsie's Hideaway, the bar at which they had originally met (59–60). It is equally impossible to fear the outcome of their crime. Consequently, the novel's theme, its message of faith and hope and love, is relatively muted. Throughout their ordeal, neither the Reillys nor the Meehans nor Rosita and Fred lose hope that goodness will prevail, and of course it does. On Christmas Eve, their ordeal behind them, love warms their spirits and gives meaning to their lives, a point that the Clarks punctuate with the promise of romance not only between Rosita and Fred but also between Regan and the New York detective who has been handling her father's case, Jack Reilly, whose surname makes him already one of the family. With every reason to be jolly, *Deck the Halls*'s characters testify to the meaning of the holiday season.

In the end, *Deck the Halls* is a light caper compared to its weightier predecessors. In those previous novels, Clark's complex characters seem genuinely at risk, and their ordeals lead them to an increased knowledge of self. Her solemn tone, moreover, underscores the meaning of the Christmas story. In collaboration with her daughter, however, whose mysteries tend toward the comic, Clark indulges her own penchant for humor, drawing characters in broad strokes, sometimes almost as caricatures, and basing the plot on inept kidnappers who are from the novel's beginning doomed to fail. The combination keeps at bay any real suspense, but it does provide a lighthearted dose of holiday cheer. *Deck the Halls*'s humor is thus at once both its strength and its weakness.

HE SEES YOU WHEN YOU'RE SLEEPING: A NOVEL (2001)

Clark clearly enjoyed her collaboration with her daughter, for she followed it a year later with another fanciful concoction, *He Sees You When You're Sleeping*. Reminiscent of its literary predecessor, Charles Dickens's *A Christmas Carol* (1843), as well as director Frank Capra's 1946 film classic *It's a Wonderful Life*, the Clarks' tale of Christmas suspense features a man who is given the chance to change his fate by changing himself. In doing so, he discovers the true meaning of not only the holiday but also life itself. Enlivened by the pair's lighthearted humor and warmed by genuine affection for their characters, *He Sees You When You're Sleeping* is a Christmas fairy tale of redemption and love. Like the holiday tune from which it takes its title, "Santa Claus Is Coming to Town," it is a gentle reminder of the unseen forces in our lives.

He Sees You When You're Sleeping's fanciful plot begins with an unusual convocation of the Heavenly Council, who have summoned before them Sterling Brooks, a man who has lingered in the celestial waiting room outside the heavenly gates for determination of his fate for forty-six years, longer than any other person. Sad and forlorn, Brooks longs for nothing more than to be granted Christmas amnesty and to enter into heaven, especially now that the woman he loved, Annie Mansfield, has gone to that place of final rest. But the Heavenly Council has a different plan for Sterling: They will give him another opportunity to earn his place in heaven.

Transported back to earth to redeem himself, Brooks lands at Rockefeller Center, where his life intersects with that of seven-year-old Marissa Campbell. The Christmas before this approaching one, Marissa had been carefree and happy, secure in the love of her mother and stepfather as well as her adored father and grandmother. At the new year, however, Marissa's father, Billy Campbell, a rising pop musician, and his mother, the popular restaurateur Nor Kelly, had suddenly and mysteriously stopped visiting their beloved daughter and grandchild, leaving the little girl as sad and forlorn as Sterling. Marissa has tried to keep faith in their absence, but weekly telephone calls are no substitute for their physical presence. Now she has decided that she will put them from her life forever if they do not return for her Christmas Eve birthday. That prospect, however, seems an impossibility because federal authorities have placed Billy and Nor into the Witness Protection Program. They intend to give incriminating evidence in an arson case, but the criminals, Junior and Eddie Badgett, have placed a contract on their lives. They have no intention whatsoever of spending their lives behind bars.

Sterling, drawn to Marissa's plight, seizes this as his opportunity to make a difference in someone's life and thereby prove his worth. To meet his challenge, he must enlist the help of the Heavenly Council to become a traveler in time and space. Then, armed with knowledge of all the situation's permutations, he must devise a plan to ensnare the villains, free the witnesses, and restore a young girl's faith in love. With Christmas Eve fast approaching, Sterling has little time to lose and none to be wrong.

Sterling Brooks, the central character of *He Sees You When You're Sleeping*, may not have been as miserly as Dickens's Ebenezer Scrooge, but there is no denying that he had been a singularly "self-absorbed" (18) man during his fifty-one years of life. When the Heavenly Council assemble to determine his fate, they recite a litany of his faults: Sterling had been "a fair-weather friend" (18), "a good-time Charlie" (19), "a cad" (19). So satisfied was he with his life that he had never made the effort to help someone in need—even when he considered doing so. Most damning of all, he had "hurt people by *not* doing things. And by making promises [he had] no intention of keeping" (18). Sterling's were sins of omission rather than commission, but they had consequences, nevertheless, for both himself and others. They had, most regrettably now for Sterling, prevented Annie, a woman faithful to him all her life, from enjoying marital happiness and the love of children. Too late he had come to realize that, because he would not commit to a wedding date, he had cheated them both of some of life's great satisfactions.

Sterling's efforts to assist Marissa, however, lead to his rehabilitation of character. The fact that he even notices her plight, for instance, speaks to a latent compassion, and the regret he feels about his treatment of Annie is evidence of a conscience. Given this opportunity to live his life again, Sterling now acts on those feelings. He had previously been unwilling to take risks, fearful, perhaps, of experiencing again the hurt and anxiety that he had known when he doubted his admission to study at Brown University (15). In fact, Sterling's whole existence had been to some extent about protecting himself from the vagaries and vicissitudes of life. But now he rushes full tilt into the fray, doing whatever is necessary to outwit the Badgetts, save Billy and Nor, and bring happiness to Marissa. He acts, moreover, not from self-interest (although his actions were at first so motivated), but from altruism, from genuine concern and care for others. Touched by their plight, he forgets his own (88), and in so doing, he not only connects to his own humanity but also earns his salvation.

The secondary characters in *He Sees You When You're Sleeping* are less fully delineated. Marissa is a precocious little girl who lives with her harried mother and earnest stepfather, both of whom provide her with the love and stability necessary to thrive. Billy Campbell and Nor Kelly are charismatic figures who bring an equal amount of love but offer an exciting alternative lifestyle to Marissa's staid existence. All are honest, upright, and deserving people with whom readers can both identify and sympathize. None of them should suffer as they do. Only the Clarks' characterization of the Badgetts is more than superficial, and here again, just as they did in *Deck the Halls,* mother and daughter turn to humor to flesh out their villains.

Brothers Junior and Eddie Badgett are, as their name suggests, bad to the core, utterly unredeemable. Having fled their native Wallonia, a tiny country bordering Albania, to avoid joining their father in prison, the Badgetts now live in an ostentatious Long Island mansion, tribute to their ability to raise a fortune from loan-sharking and pyramid schemes—as well as their bad taste. Hard as nails about everything except their eighty-five-year-old mother, Heddy-Anna, over whom they cry copious tears about their separation, the brothers rely on fear and intimidation to coerce hapless borrowers such as Hans Kramer and honest employees such as Billy and Nor into submission. They have even ensnared their lawyer, Charlie Santoli, who intended to do nothing more than handle their legitimate business (55), in their criminal net. The Badgetts fear little from authorities, who have tried without success to prosecute them, for their money, after all, gives them the clout to command mayors, boards of governors, and even senators to celebrate their absent mother's birthday. Surely it will buy them protection as well.

Their ability to have Hans Kramer's warehouse set fire when he seeks an extension of his loan payment and to place a contract on Billy's and Nor's lives for their insistence on giving evidence against them makes the Badgetts genuine menaces, unlike the inept criminals in *Deck the Halls.* Yet the novel's humor, as it did in that previous work, effectively diminishes the sense of any real threat. It is hard, for instance, to fear criminals referred to as "the baseball bat and the bowling ball brothers" (5), harder still when they are so easily outwitted by their crafty mother. Each time her devoted sons telephone, she secures gifts and money by reciting a litany of health problems from a list posted on the wall, often simultaneously tucking into a thick bowl of stew to feed her robust appetite for living. By the time Junior and Eddie don monks' habits and sandals for what they believe will be a tearful reunion with their mother at the St. Stephen of the Mountain monastery, they are little more than laughing-stocks. In fact, it is hard to believe that they could ever have threatened anyone.

The Clarks clearly enjoyed creating their lighthearted caper, for they developed some outrageous set pieces that have as much to do with play-ing for laughs as they do with advancing the novel's plot. Chief among them is the delightful scene in which mama Heddy-Anna, who has just hauled and unloaded a cartful of logs at her house, waits for a telephone call from her sons while she and ten friends laugh and gossip over a hearty meal and good wine (143–48). Equally comic is the novel's opening scene, where members of the Heavenly Council, a disparate group of four men and four women wearing the clothing typical of the period in which they had lived and including everyone from a monk and a matador to a woman resembling Pocahontas and a saint dressed in the uniform of a British admiral, interrogate Sterling in contemporary slang and jargon (17–21). The incongruity of a monk informing Sterling, "We've got a bone to pick with you" (17), a shepherd accusing him of being "a fair-weather friend" (18), and the whole council agreeing, "That's it in a nutshell" (19) is enough to elicit a laugh from most readers. So, too, is the scene in which the Badgett brothers, travelling as Brother Stanislas and Brother Casper, make their pilgrimage to mama Heddy-Anna on a plane full of federal agents disguised as nuns and priests (191–94). These comic turns substi-tute to some extent for the suspense typical of a Mary Higgins Clark novel, for they do indeed diminish that element of *He Sees You When You're Sleeping*.

The Clarks' humor, however, does not diminish the significance of their themes. In Sterling Brooks, mother and daughter give readers an Every-man, someone like them who on his journey through life must choose the proper path. Sterling, they make clear, chose wrongly. He was not a bad man and certainly not a criminal, but he neglected his human obligations. As the monk on the Heavenly Council explains, "Too many people were invisible to him" (68), so he could easily ignore their needs. Smug and self-satisfied, he failed to acknowledge that he purchased at least a portion of his ease and comfort with Annie's sacrifices. Who knows who paid for the remainder? Sterling's first lesson, then, which he clearly takes to heart, is "to learn to recognize people's needs and to do something about them" (21). It is a lesson intended for readers as well.

The second lesson readers take from Sterling's example is that it is never too late to change course on life's journey. That lesson the Clarks reinforce in the example of Charlie Santoli, the Badgetts' lawyer. Charlie had never intended to become involved in his clients' criminal affairs. All he had ever wanted were the large fees they would pay for handling their legitimate business. Too late, however, he finds himself intimidating potential witnesses against his clients, fearful for his life should he try to quit working for them (55), and filled with self-loathing for what he has become (108). The Heavenly Council justifiably frets about Charlie's future (111), but then the beleaguered lawyer gets some unexpected help. Sterling, recognizing that Charlie does indeed, as the nurse on the Heavenly Council claims, "[want] to be good" (111), enlists his assistance with the plan he has devised to entice the Badgetts to Wallonia, and Charlie readily agrees to help. Given his own second chance, Charlie, like Sterling, chooses a different path and so redeems his life.

By Christmas Eve, when *He Sees You When You're Sleeping* ends, Sterling has indeed earned his reward in heaven. He has not only reunited Marissa with her father and grandmother, restoring her faith in goodness and love, but also rescued Charlie from his "destructive life" (201). In listening to his heart, Sterling has discovered the joy of bringing happiness to others. He has learned, in other words, the true meaning of the holiday season. It is, perhaps, the most important lesson in the Clarks' Christmas fable.

Mary Higgins Clark certainly serves up holiday treats to her many fans in her tales of Christmas suspense. All the elements that they have come to expect in her fiction—a plot full of complications, a cast of sympathetic characters, enough suspense to experience a not unpleasant sense of menace, and a satisfying ending that rewards goodness and restores order— are here, and made, perhaps, more poignant than usual by their seasonal setting. The Christmas holiday is not, after all, the time to worry about anything more pressing than which tie to give to dad, which scent to buy for mom. Clark's tales, however, remind readers of the dark realities that colored lights and tinsel merely camouflage. Then they offer their own messages of faith in humanity. Like the songs and carols from which they take their titles, Clark's tales of Christmas suspense celebrate peace and joy and love and remind everyone of what is truly important in life.

5

Moonlight Becomes You
(1996)

When death visits the halls of a retirement residence, even an impeccably tasteful and genteel manor house for the wealthy in Newport, Rhode Island, its presence is a sad but inevitable reminder of human mortality. Murder, however, is another matter altogether, and to Nuala Moore, murder is exactly what the series of sudden deaths at Latham Manor is beginning to seem. Nuala unfortunately never has the opportunity to share her suspicions because she herself is viciously bludgeoned to death in her comfortable home, but that act is a killer's undoing in Mary Higgins Clark's thirteenth best-selling novel of mystery and suspense, *Moonlight Becomes You*. Nuala's murder becomes the basis for a tightly plotted and intriguing tale of greed and grief that is grounded in the legacy of the past. It is familiar Clark territory, but with a few subtle twists, the "Queen of Suspense" makes it seem a foreign country. Readers will be glad they booked a trip.

Moonlight Becomes You reunites the fashion photographer Maggie Holloway with her former stepmother Nuala Moore after a twenty-two-year separation. Eager to renew a relationship that each had valued, Maggie accepts Nuala's invitation to spend several weeks visiting with her at her Newport home, so when she arrives a week later to find her former stepmother lying dead in the living room, her preparations for a homecoming dinner party clearly interrupted by an intruder, she is devastated. Her grief soon mingles with disbelief when she learns that Nuala had changed her will the day before her death, canceling the sale of her house to her lawyer, Malcolm Norton, and leaving the bulk of her estate to Maggie. Convinced by these sudden revelations that something had been troubling Nuala prior to her death, something that had also prompted her former stepmother to cancel her plans to take up residence in Latham Manor, Maggie determines to conduct her own investigation of Nuala's life. Her sleuthing leads to the discovery of an elaborate cast-iron bell buried in the rich earth around the headstone of Nuala's grave. When she finds identical bells on the graves of three of Nuala's recently deceased friends, each of whom had been a resident of Latham Manor, Maggie is convinced that her former stepmother's murder had not been a random act. That conviction will eventually lead to her own encounter with a killer who does not wait this time until his victim is dead to place a funeral bell on her grave.

PLOT

Clark begins her novel at its conclusion. Maggie has been buried alive by a killer who, as readers learn when Clark eventually returns to the scene, intends to taunt her prior to her death. Entombed within a Victorian casket that has a breathing tube as well as a funeral bell, testament to that generation's fear of premature burial, Maggie has some hope of survival. She pulls on the string attached to her finger, jerking the bell back and forth in its *"arrhythmic dance of death"* (3). But readers know what Maggie does not—the bell's clapper has been removed. From that moment, the novel's tense suspense begins. Despite her frantic attempts to alert someone to her predicament, Maggie, it seems certain, is doomed to die. Readers, of course, must now race through an account of the events preceding this incident, not only to place it in context, but also to learn its outcome. From such a beginning Clark propels her readers into a macabre and fearsome world.

The remainder of Clark's novel follows a linear plot structure organized around a calendar of events. That calendar provides *Moonlight Becomes You* with the time constraints that serve as Clark's typical strategy for building suspense. Readers know that Maggie lies in her coffin on Tuesday, October 8. The events preceding that day begin on Friday, September 20. In a period of less than three weeks, Maggie's life has clearly collapsed. That it could have spun out of control so quickly is testament to the terror and menace that must have occurred during that time.

Clark may begin her novel at its most suspenseful point, but she modulates and controls her pace as well as her tone in *Moonlight Becomes You*'s first real-time chapter, which is set on Friday, September 20, at a family celebration, a cocktail party to honor the anniversary of the 115th birthday of Squire Desmond Moore, the Moore family patriarch. A festive affair enlivened by a host of relatives regaling each other with family myths and legends, it seems hardly the beginning for a novel of suspense. Moreover, it is an unlikely setting for the reunion of Maggie and Nuala because neither, it transpires, is a Moore family member. Nuala attends as Tim Moore's widow—and because she is such a merry and vivacious creature that the family still holds her close. Maggie attends this family reunion, against her better judgment, as the guest of Liam Moore Payne, Tim Moore's nephew. When they find each other, everything seems suddenly right for both. The joy of their serendipitous meeting, however, is merely a brief prelude to far more serious matters. One week later, on Friday, September 27, at what should have been Maggie's homecoming party, Nuala lies dead on the floor, and Maggie's nightmare begins. The contrast between this second celebratory occasion and the first shifts Clark's suspense once again, and from this point it never flags.

This second celebratory event also serves as a brilliant plot device by which to introduce the novel's list of suspects, for it soon becomes obvious that Nuala's killer must have been one of the guests. Her house, after all, shows no signs of forced entry. Moreover, only someone who knew the time at which her guests, including Maggie, were due to arrive would have risked ransacking her home when it was clear from the boiling potatoes and roasting lamb that Nuala was expecting company. On her guest list, then, is the name of a killer. Liam Moore Payne and his cousin Earl Bateman, both of whom had been present at their founder's celebration; Dr. William Lane, director of Latham Manor, and his wife Odile; Nuala's attorney, Malcolm Norton, and his wife Janice, the bookkeeper at Latham Manor, had all been expected to dine at Nuala's home and to meet her former stepdaughter. The fact that the killer was someone she trusted enough to invite into her home makes the murder doubly insidious.

While a predator from within seemingly narrows the scope of the investigation and in consequence it would seem the novel's plot, Clark includes several important subplots that call into question that initial conclusion. The death of Greta Shipley, for instance, less than a week after her friend Nuala's murder, seems at first a sad coincidence, but Maggie soon discovers that Greta was one of several residents of Latham Manor who had died after brief and sudden illnesses. Such information might seem to incriminate the Lanes, but it also adds to the suspect list Nurse Zelda Markey, whose habit of intruding on Latham Manor's residents had made Greta suspicious of her. Another subplot concerning investment fraud introduces an additional suspect, Douglas Hansen, and provides Clark the opportunity to bring Maggie's love interest, Neil Stephens, into the novel's action. Hansen, a charmer who peddles risky investments to elderly women too flattered by his attentions to question either his integrity or his knowledge, had victimized two of Robert Stephens' clients, and the lawyer and financial advisor enlists the help of his son Neil during a visit to his parents' Newport home to salvage some of their assets. In the course of their investigation, the Stephenses will discover Hansen's connections to both Janice Norton and Latham Manor, connections that further complicate the novel's primary plot.

While all leads seem to point to Latham Manor as the key to the novel's mystery, Clark manages one other feat of misdirection to keep her plot from unraveling too soon. The Bateman Funeral Museum, which houses Earl Bateman's eerie collection of death paraphernalia, including the mysterious cast-iron bells that Maggie discovers on the graves of Nuala and her friends, certainly seems as if it must be connected to these deaths, especially because readers know that Maggie is buried alive in a Victorian casket that could only have come from Bateman's. The museum clearly throws the weight of suspicion on its equally eerie creator, and so for much of the novel it diverts readers from much consideration of the true criminal. Granted, Bateman seems too obvious a suspect from the novel's beginning, but in the absence of any other real probability, Clark's ploy seems to be to make readers finally suspect the obvious, a strategy that demonstrates her skill at manipulating all the elements of the genre.

CHARACTER DEVELOPMENT

Bateman seems the most plausible suspect because Clark delineates his character in such detail. An anthropology professor at Hutchinson College in Providence, Rhode Island, Earl Bateman is also a lecturer on funeral customs through the ages. He may not have entered the family business, but in his own way, he has. In fact, he is, as his cousin Liam tells Maggie, "obsessed with the subject of death" (72). His pride in his funeral museum confirms that assessment. Bateman is clearly an odd case. Not only does he seem more at ease with the dead, but he also harbors a great deal of resentment toward his Moore family connections. Although the Bateman wealth is far greater than the Moore fortune, Earl is aware that "the Moore clan call him 'Cousin Weirdo'" (260), so he wants desperately to secure their respect, particularly Liam's. When his cousin comes for drinks, Earl casually leaves a three thousand dollar check, the honorarium for a speaking engagement, lying on the bar to elicit Liam's praise. The smooth investment manager, however, ignores the bait, just as, readers suspect, he would probably ignore any Bateman success, including the proposed television series about funeral customs that Earl is convinced will bring him the recognition he deserves. Everything about Earl—his obsession with death, his resentment of his family, his lack of self-worth, his need for recognition—makes his interest in Maggie a threat. When he begins to visit her unannounced at Nuala's house, it seems inevitable that threat will soon escalate into incident.

The rivalry between Earl Bateman and his utterly self-assured cousin, Liam Moore Payne, never seems more than a one-sided affair in Clark's novel. Charming and clever, Liam is head of his own successful investment firm in Boston. His date with Maggie at the Moore family celebration suggests his ease with women. Liam, it seems, could want nothing that Earl possesses, and the fond bemusement with which he treats his cousin simply reinforces that perception. Liam, however, conceals his true nature beneath his good looks and manners. Too late, Maggie recognizes "the superficial smile, the calculated sincerity, the practiced warmth" (326) that have deceived everyone about Liam. As obsessed with his family legacy as Earl is obsessed with his, Liam dreams of being "the second Squire Moore" (328), a man whose "god *was* money" (114), so while he may appear indifferent to his cousin's wealth, he is secretly jealous of it and contemptuous of the man who uses it so pitifully. In fact, he seems even to have adopted the Squire's view that "it was more interesting to cheat someone out of [his money] than make it honestly" (337), since his business success suggests that he has the ability to earn his fortune honestly. It is clearly Liam's obsession rather than Earl's that is lethal.

Clark delineates her novel's other suspects with attention to detail, providing each with a plausible motive for murder. Dr. William Lane, for instance, the director of Latham Manor, owes his position to his wife, Odile, a beautiful but seemingly vacuous woman who never misses an opportunity to remind him of the fact. An inept physician who is just managing to keep in check a drinking problem, he feels trapped in his marriage and pressured by his employers to keep every room at Latham Manor fully occupied, so Nuala's cancellation of her contract to enter the facility is another worrisome problem for him. Malcolm Norton, Nuala's lawyer, also has reason to kill. Like Lane, he is trapped in a loveless marriage with a woman who never lets him forget that he is a failure. In love now with his secretary, Barbara Hoffman, a principled woman who will not begin a relationship with him until he is free, he has devised a plan for achieving his desires: Armed with inside information about her property, he will purchase Nuala's house at a price less than its potential value and then sell it for a huge profit when the removal of wetlands restrictions makes it ripe for development. The profit will free him from Janice and ensure his happiness with Barbara. Norton, however, is a man "destined to wander forever through a field of broken dreams" (74), and Nuala's cancellation of the sale of her house to him leaves him not with a windfall profit but a two hundred thousand dollar second mortgage on his home—as well as Janice's bitter contempt. Janice, for her part, is engaging in some sort of swindle involving her nephew Douglas Hansen and Latham Manor, so she may have had her own reasons for killing Nuala. With reason to hate or to fear Nuala, Clark's suspects are all plausible murderers because they are all in fact criminals. Greed, envy, bitterness, and hate have twisted them until only self-interest matters. Anyone who stands in their way is at risk.

Nuala's death at the hands of one of her guests might not say much for her judgment of people. Nor would her five-year marriage to Maggie's father, Owen Holloway, a hard and critical man who could not see beyond the dirty dishes in the kitchen sink or the clutter in a desk drawer to appreciate his wife's generous and loving spirit. Yet the very trust and sincerity that may have contributed to her murder also made her a formidable presence, someone whose undaunted spirit and insatiable zest for living demanded notice. She had been Maggie's childhood champion, and she had died because she could not ignore the mysterious circumstances surrounding her friends' deaths. She was, in many ways, a woman well suited to her name, Finnuala, a female Finn MacCool, the legendary hero who defeated a giant in Celtic mythology (10).

Nuala's five years as Maggie's stepmother were certainly important to the young girl. Maggie had never known her own mother, who had died in an automobile accident when her daughter was an infant, so she had come to love as a mother the woman who had encouraged her artistic talents and nurtured her developing sense of self until her difficult and disapproving father drove her from their lives. When circumstance unexpectedly reunites them, the twenty-two intervening years between them simply slip away over cocktails and confidences at Maggie's favorite restaurant, to which they have gone to escape the Moore celebration. As the novel develops, it becomes clear that Maggie owes more than her love of sculpting and her skill at photography to her former stepmother.

Like Nuala, Maggie is honest and forthright, so she trusts what she sees in others. A woman of her word, she visits Greta Shipley because Nuala had requested in her will that she do so, but genuine compassion for and interest in others lead her to befriend the elderly woman and to gain the respect of Letitia Bainbridge, who observes that Maggie, unlike so many of the young, is not "indifferent [to] or impatient with old fossils like me" (303). Maggie, like all of Clark's typical heroines, personifies goodness, so she deserves every good thing that has come her way. At one level, she even deserves it because her life has not been perfect. Like the lives of other Clark heroines, Maggie's past has its share of pain, and the young woman wrestles still with sadness. This aspect of her character provides the basis for one of the novel's central themes, or main ideas.

THEMATIC ISSUES

The legacy of the past lies at the heart of *Moonlight Becomes You*. The examples of Earl Bateman and Liam Moore Payne certainly speak to this point. Each of these men has been shaped by family heritage. Earl is every bit an undertaker's son, despite his academic position. People's general discomfort with death has made this undertaker's son an outsider, even within his own extended family, so Earl wants nothing more than the recognition and respect that will signify acceptance to him. Liam, too, is the product of his past. Squire Desmond Moore, the family's venerated rogue, is his ideal self-image, and he is willing to lie, cheat, steal, and even murder to achieve his dream of attaining that man's stature. Each of these men becomes what he is as a consequence of his past, and so, too, does Maggie Holloway. Her past, like theirs, is an undiscovered country awaiting exploration. But it must be explored, Clark makes clear, if she is to move forward into the future. This truth is central to Clark's examination of the legacy of the past.

Unresolved grief lies in Maggie Holloway's past, but the murder of her former stepmother forces her to acknowledge and come to terms with it. For five years, Nuala had been the mother Maggie had never known. When her stern and demanding father criticized his daughter's behavior or dress, Nuala would take Maggie's part, defending her need to be herself. Then suddenly she was gone from her life, leaving Maggie with a sense of abandonment that her father's interception of Nuala's letters to her fuelled. Twenty-two years later, just as fortune gives them the opportunity to renew their relationship, Maggie discovers Nuala's battered body. Grief leads her back in memory, and soon, Nuala's death is helping

Maggie to heal from another great loss in her life, the death of her husband, Paul, five years before.

Although Maggie had "mentioned matter-of-factly" to Neil Stephens on one of their first dates her widowed state, "her tone suggesting," he had concluded, "that emotionally she had put that behind her" (31), a subsequent incident calls into question his conclusion. Recognizing Maggie seated a few rows in front of him at a matinee screening of *A Man and a Woman* several months before, he realizes as well that she is stifling sobs as she watches the story of "a young widow who could not accept her husband's death" (32). While Neil may have again misjudged Maggie's reaction, it is certainly true that Maggie grieves still for her husband. Stored in a box in her closet is the dress she had worn on the night they met "as well as one of his [Air Force] flight suits and their matching jogging outfits" (192). Earl Bateman had also sensed that Maggie is not "close to *anyone*" (107), an observation that suggests deliberate avoidance of more than casual relationships. As she sets to right Nuala's house and estate, she finds herself wishing that Nuala, who had herself been widowed young, were there to listen to her story. She would have told her former stepmother of her efforts to stop time, of the hairstyle and cosmetics that she had continued to wear for five years after Paul's death because he had preferred them that way, and of her recent makeover. "She would have understood," Maggie thinks (92), revealing her confusion and guilt about her tentative passage into the future.

Nuala, however, even in death, does become Maggie's confidant. As she takes possession of her former stepmother's house, Maggie senses in the spirit of the place Nuala's spirit, and she takes comfort in it. Nuala had loved and had gone on loving, Maggie realizes, as she leafs through her former stepmother's photograph albums. Nuala had known joy and happiness even after her divorce from Maggie's father and her beloved husband's death. Like Nuala, Maggie, too, can pack away her "grief equipment" (247) and have such a future. Indeed, she has already begun to claim it. The hurt she feels about Neil's seeming indifference to her is certainly one sign that her heart has begun to heal. Moreover, for the first time since Paul's death, she is "nesting" (202), a term that suggests the creation of a nurturing space from which springs new life. When Maggie escapes her premature burial, she is essentially reborn, ready for the new love and the new life that await her.

Clark emphasizes the need to face the pain of loss and the anger and guilt of survival that accompany death by imbuing her tale with funeral lore and traditions. One of the clues to the killer's identity is an elaborate cast-iron bell that Maggie finds buried on Nuala's grave and the graves of others who, she comes to believe, have also been murder victims. Her search for the bell's meaning leads to her discovery of the Victorian custom of vented caskets topped by a bell which the deceased could ring by pulling a string to alert others should he or she have been buried alive. It leads her as well to the Bateman Funeral Museum, where Earl treats her to a tour of the memorabilia of "grief culture" (246). Among the funeral customs that Clark relates to readers throughout the novel is the impropriety of speaking the words "dead," "killed," or "dies," as if to deny the reality and finality of death (106). Another is the traditional banquet or feast following a funeral, one of many "separation rites" intended to ease the pain of loss because "a diverse people inherently understood that . . . extended grief is debilitating to the individual and the community" (248). That sentiment, which is reiterated in the advice of the researcher Durkheim that Bateman quotes to Maggie—"Sorrow like joy becomes exalted and amplified when leaping from mind to mind" (52), Clark clearly shares. In fact, she enlists all of this seemingly arcane information in *Moonlight Becomes You* to make just that point.

Whatever its source, Clark makes clear with all of these examples, the legacy of the past exerts a powerful effect on the present. That effect, however, need not be harmful. So long as people recognize its influence, so long as they face the past, in other words, they have the power to live with it. They may even gain strength from facing it. This theme clearly strikes a chord for Clark, who explores it in many of her novels. It certainly rings true as well in a novel of mystery and suspense, where the revelation of secrets, generally from the past, is always one of the outcomes of the plot.

The monstrous nature of greed is the secondary theme of *Moonlight Becomes You*. Greed perverts the humanity of Liam Moore Payne, Malcolm and Janice Norton, Douglas Hansen, and even Odile Lane, making them selfish predators who disregard the rights and even the integrity of others. For the sake of profit, Malcolm Norton, Nuala's lawyer, had been quite willing to betray years of trust and cheat a woman of the real value of her property. For lucrative remuneration, Janice Norton and Douglas Hansen had conspired with Liam Moore Payne to defraud unsuspecting elderly women of their life savings. For the sake of a dream of amassing a fortune, Liam Moore Payne had orchestrated a plot that included murder without the least twinge of guilt and had enlisted Odile Lane's equally remorseless assistance. Money is the root of evil in *Moonlight Becomes You*. It perverts goodness and compassion, trust and honor. It even makes criminals of some and victims of others. So many greedy people fill the world of *Moonlight Becomes You* that Clark is clearly taking aim at a problem that debases human society.

A MARXIST READING OF *MOONLIGHT BECOMES YOU*

By placing money at the center of her novel's plot, Clark provides the Marxist critic with some provocative evidence by which to examine class issues in *Moonlight Becomes You*. Such a critic focuses on the relation between literature and history, emphasizing particularly the social and economic factors that, according to the German philosopher Karl Marx (1818–1883), drive historical change. Like feminism, with which it shares certain basic principles, Marxism is not a single theory. In fact, several different schools of Marxist critics exist, and "all of them," according to Arthur Asa Berger, "base their criticism on varying and sometimes conflicting interpretations of Marx's theories and how they can be applied to analyzing culture in general and, more specifically, literary texts, works of elite culture, popular culture, and the mass media" (41). To understand Marxist criticism, then, we need first to explain briefly the concepts that serve as its foundation.

Marx is usually classified as a "dialectical materialist." He believed that historical transformations occur through a dialectic, or development, through the stages of thesis, antithesis, and synthesis. Each historical force, according to Marx, calls into being its Other so that the two opposing forces negate each other and eventually give rise to a third force that transcends its opposition. Unlike his great teacher Hegel, who was an idealist, Marx was a materialist who believed that social forces shape human consciousness.

For Marx, the ultimate moving force of human history is economics, or perhaps more specifically, political economy. This term encompasses political and social issues as well as economic factors. Each society, according to Marx, bases its culture upon its means of production, the techniques by which it produces food, clothing, shelter, and other necessities of life, and the social relations these methods create. For example, an economy based on manufacturing demands a division of labor, cooperation among workers, and a hierarchical system of managers. These economic demands in turn shape the social relations of the people. From this basic premise, Marx argued that major historical changes occur as a result of economic contradictions, what might be termed class consciousness and class conflict. Conflict between the aristocracy and the middle classes, for example, was the source of the French Revolution of the 1790s.

In Marxist thought, the economic base gives rise to and shapes the superstructure, which finds expression in the culture's ideology, its collective consciousness of itself. This ideology comprises all the institutions of the society, such as the church, the education system, the art world, and the legal system. The ideology, which includes literature, generally conforms to and supports the culture's dominant means of production. Economic conditions alone, however, are not sufficient to explain the development and effect of its institutions. Human agency, or individual consciousness, is active in these institutions as well. Thus, Marxist criticism that focuses exclusively on economics and that celebrates the proletariat, or working class, has been termed "vulgar Marxism" for its crude tendency to oversimplify complex issues.

Marxism is primarily a political and economic philosophy, not a guide to understanding literature. As a result, Marxist criticism takes a variety of forms, depending upon how the text is defined in relation to material reality or to ideology. Clark's presentation of a privileged elite in Newport, Rhode Island, a retreat for wealthy Americans since the nineteenth century, lends itself most readily to a Marxist critique based upon the reflection theory. As an imitation of the culture that helped to produce it, the novel dramatizes the forces, both psychological and social, that lie behind criminal behavior. For the Marxist critic, a significant aspect of them all is class consciousness and class conflict.

Moonlight Becomes You's Newport setting is certainly significant to an understanding of its class issues. Clark takes great care to render its historic mansions, those "relics of a bygone age" that still bring tourists to gape at their wonders (15), in all their extravagant grandeur. The Breakers, for instance, built for Cornelius Vanderbilt II and his wife, Alice, is the community's "most marvelously ostentatious jewel," an "American palace" that testifies to "what money, and imagination, and driving ambition could achieve" (16). The former Ochre Court, which now houses a university, is a "hundred-room extravagance" standing "splendid against the skyline," while Latham Manor is a "worthy, [but] more tasteful competitor to the vulgarity of The Breakers" (16). These mansions housed a privileged few who flaunted their wealth and were the envy of ordinary people. A hundred years later, tourists still pay homage to these symbols of an American elite, and people such as Greta Shipley and Letitia Bainbridge testify to that elite's continued existence. After all, the average person cannot afford the one-quarter to one-half million dollar fee for an apartment at Latham Manor. In a democratic United States, these mansions make clear, where all citizens no matter what their income consider themselves middle-class, class divisions definitely did and do exist.

It was class divisions, in fact, that prompted these mansions' original owners to marry their daughters into titled English families. As Letitia Bainbridge tells Maggie, "Poor Consuelo Vanderbilt—her mother threatened to commit suicide if she didn't marry the Duke of Marlborough" (113). She eventually submitted to her parents' will, but only found happiness twenty years later after she divorced Marlborough and married a French intellectual. Consuelo's story was common among America's nouveau riche, people who had money without cachet, without the hereditary legitimacy conferred by a title and the proper social connections. Feeling this inadequacy, they erected their American palaces to prove their worth and sold their daughters to secure their social standing. The system worked because England's impoverished nobility were willing to trade their good names for an American fortune, however it was made (114).

It was class divisions as well that created the original Squire Desmond Moore. When the fifteen-year-old immigrant from Ireland's Dingle peninsula arrived on America's shores, he considered himself "not one of the huddled masses yearning to be free but, rather, one of the impoverished masses yearning to be rich" (6), and he set out to make his fortune however he could. By the time of his death, this "fixture of Newport society" (6) had been capable of building residences for each of his seven children (23), but as Letitia Bainbridge tells Maggie, "Everyone knew he came from nothing" (114). The squire may have claimed to be a direct descendant of the Irish hero Brian Boru, but his title was probably "pretense" (114). Every detail about his history suggests that Squire Moore was acutely aware of class distinctions and that at some level this self-made millionaire felt his own inadequacy against the cachet of inherited position.

Years later, Squire Moore's sense of inadequacy will surface in his descendants, Liam Moore Payne and Earl Bateman. Liam, of course, has dreamed of being "the second Squire Moore," with the wealth and power to establish a dynasty, but his failure prompts him to admit that he is "just another failed Moore" (328), an allusion perhaps to the fact that "the Batemans could buy and sell most of the Moores" (260). Liam, in other words, is aware that the Moore heritage had always been more pretense than fact and at some level resents the truth—and his cousin, a man whom he clearly holds in contempt and believes undeserving of his fortune.

Earl, for his part, cannot overcome his sense of inferiority. Squire Moore had never approved his daughter's marriage to Gordon Bateman because he feared reminders of his mortality. Years later, his descendents still mock their strange cousin and treat him as an inferior member of the clan. Earl takes some pleasure in the Bateman family revenge: In "mocking tribute to his father-in-law," Gordon Bateman had convinced his wife to name their house, the smallest of any presented to his children, Squire Hall (23). He also believes that his name had been a deliberate "jab" at Squire: "A squire in Dingle," after all, "tugged his forelock in homage to an earl" (23). His own family wealth and status, nevertheless, are not enough to convince Earl of his value. The family hierarchy has thus been a source of disappointment for both of Squire Moore's descendants.

In Newport's class-conscious world, the hierarchies created by money, power, and privilege breed envy, contempt, and discontent among all populations. Competition for certain coveted rooms at Latham Manor, for instance, at least in part makes necessary Liam Moore Payne's murderous plot. Eleanor Chandler, whose grandmother had been "one of Newport's social grandes dames during the city's social zenith in the 1890s," is the ideal candidate for residence at Latham Manor (93), but she is adamant in her refusal to accept any other apartment than Greta Shipley's. Within days, of course, Greta is dead, and rumor has it that Mrs. Chandler's name has gone to the top of the waiting list for her apartment. Prestige is clearly the selling point of Prestige Residence Corporation, Latham Manor's parent company, and thus its very existence occasionally depends upon its clients' desires to validate their sense of superiority but especially upon its need to enhance its own image through its clientele.

The example of Malcolm and Janice Norton also testifies to the subversive effect of class consciousness and class divisions. Malcolm may be a "blue [blood] with [a] lineage [he] could trace back past the Mayflower to the aristocracy" (74), but his patrician background has simply made him the "ultimate Ken doll" (74), a handsome but ineffectual man. Thirty-five years of marriage to such a man have made Janice a bitter woman, especially because through the years she has had to watch her classmates make brilliant marriages. At Greta Shipley's funeral, Janice is made "freshly and bitterly aware of the financial gap" that separates her from others in her community and thinks with disgust that Regina Carr Wayne, who had married the CEO and chief stockholder of a pharmaceutical firm, "was not an accountant in an old-folks home" (197). Filled with "loathing" for her husband (197) and bitterness and self-pity for her situation, Janice feels justified in defrauding Latham Manor's potential residents. After all, "they had never known a day's worry about money" (74). Her unspoken assumption is that neither should she have known one.

For the Marxist critic, the various examples of social hierarchy in *Moonlight Becomes You* are clear evidence of a fundamental inequity in America that is at odds with its basic principles of equality. One of the essential American myths is the self-made man. Anyone, so the myth goes, by dint of hard work and personal effort, can rise to the top of society. Indeed, anyone regardless of background can one day become president. American history is full of examples from Abraham Lincoln to Bill Clinton that fuel the myth. In truth, however, the fortunes of birth and marriage have as much, if not more, effect on status and success as personal achievement and merit. The rich, in other words, get richer because they are rich. Although some of Latham Manor's residents have earned their price of admission through hard work and personal effort, the majority, Janice Norton discovers to her bitter frustration, "had been born sucking on the proverbial silver spoon" (74). The vast majority of society, in contrast, struggles simply not to live meanly, and even those who do succeed beyond the many never achieve full acceptance in the upper echelons of the social order.

Class is clearly the unspoken reality of American society. *Moonlight Becomes You*, however, exposes not only its existence but also its effect. Class divisions and class consciousness once transformed Consuelo Vanderbilt into a valuable commodity on the marriage market. A century later, they still have the power to undermine the self-esteem of Earl Bateman and to make criminals of Liam Moore Payne and Janice Norton as well as others. Internal factors, character flaws and weaknesses, certainly play their part in human behavior, but social systems, the Marxist critic would insist, also have their effect. A hierarchical system inevitably leads to invidious comparison and ruthless competition. It inevitably leads to misplaced values that justify inhumane and immoral behavior. It inevitably fosters a world of Newports, in other words, communities that conceal behind their splendid façades the class distinctions that uphold them as well as threaten to destroy them. For the Marxist critic, *Moonlight Becomes You* is clearly a cautionary tale about the American class system.

Such an interpretation certainly casts a different light on Clark's examination of the nature of greed in *Moonlight Becomes You*, but it does not invalidate her point. The novel's range and depth can, in fact, encompass both perspectives as well as her analysis of grief and the legacy of the past. *Moonlight Becomes You* is clearly a novel rich in ideas, and Clark does justice to them all through her handling of its various plot threads and her development of its cast of characters. *Moonlight Becomes You* is Mary Higgins Clark at her best.

6

Pretend You Don't See Her
(1997)

Questions of identity loom large in Mary Higgins Clark's fourteenth best-selling novel of mystery and suspense, 1997's *Pretend You Don't See Her*. Some are quite prosaic. Who, for instance, murdered Isabelle Waring, the grieving mother of the aspiring actress Heather Landi, who had herself recently died in an auto accident? Who took aim at Lacey Farrell, the only witness to the murder, prompting her disappearance into the Federal Witness Protection Program? Who stole Heather's journal, with its potentially damaging information, from police custody? Others are more profound, especially the novel's key thematic questions: Who is Alice Carroll, and what is her relationship to Lacey Farrell? The answers to all of these questions give shape and meaning to *Pretend You Don't See Her*.

When Lacey Farrell, a rising star on Manhattan's competitive real estate scene, inadvertently witnesses a client's murder and becomes guardian of a journal that could implicate others in a previous killing, she is suddenly both a suspect and a victim in *Pretend You Don't See Her*. To honor the dying wish of her client, Isabelle Waring, Lacey removes from the crime scene the journal that Isabelle's daughter, Heather Landi, had been keeping prior to her death on an icy road in Vermont. Isabelle had never believed Heather's death was an accident, and she begs Lacey to read the journal and to give it to Heather's father, the restaurateur and casino owner Jimmy Landi, that they might discover the truth about her daughter's death. Within hours of Isabelle's murder, someone has ransacked

Lacey's apartment, and police are threatening to prosecute the estate agent for withholding evidence. They are wondering as well about her relationship with her former client. When Lacey's four-year-old niece, Bonnie, takes a bullet intended for her aunt and police identify the burglar as Sandy Savarano, an enforcer for a drug cartel who they now realize had staged his death two years before, authorities begin to understand the implications of Isabelle's murder. They then give Lacey, the only person who can identify Savarano, two choices: To go into protective custody or to enter the Federal Witness Protection Program. Lacey chooses the second option.

Several months later, "Alice Carroll" arrives in Minneapolis, Minnesota, ready to begin a new life following a painful romance in Hartford, Connecticut. Before long, she has furnished an apartment, joined a health club, found a job in a real estate office, and begun to date Tom Lynch, the popular radio anchorman on WCIV. The surface of her life, however, is an elaborate deception intended to conceal her true identity, even from her loving family, and such deceptions inevitably take their toll on everyone. Despite her best intentions, "Alice" seeks to reassure her mother about her safety and tells her where she is living. This mistake brings the killer to Minneapolis and prompts Lacey to flee to New York, determined to save herself and reclaim her life because nobody else, it seems, can do it for her.

PLOT

In the Acknowledgments to *Pretend You Don't See Her*, Mary Higgins Clark explains that a song made popular by Jerry Vale, "Pretend You Don't See Her," was the inspiration for her story. The lyrics, which suggest a deliberately unseen presence, caused a plot possibility to "[crystallize]" in her mind: "A young woman witnesses a murder and to save her life has to go into the Witness Protection Program" (vii). This initial concept indicates the dual threads of the novel's plot. One thread focuses on a murder mystery, the solution of which will resolve the second thread, a mystery of identity in the larger, metaphysical sense. What is it, that second thread asks, that constitutes a self? Clark develops both of these threads in *Pretend You Don't See Her* to varying degrees of success.

As a murder mystery, *Pretend You Don't See Her* is rather frustrating, chiefly because Clark fails to play fair in her use of the conventions of the genre. Part of the mystery's appeal for readers is the intellectual challenge of matching wits with the detective or the police to solve the crime on their own from evidence in the case. Thus, the author must give readers all the clues, but without, of course, making them obvious. It is not fair to withhold a crucial piece of evidence or to conceal a suspect, but Clark certainly does the latter in this novel. Granted, she creates a cast of suspects for the murder of Heather Landi, which is, in fact, the key to Isabelle Waring's murder. Yet only one of those suspects, Rick Parker, seems probable. Parker, after all, had concealed his relationship with Heather Landi from the police, and his presence at the Vermont ski resort at which Heather had been staying prior to her death had caused her great distress. The other suspects, in contrast, seem highly improbable. Lacey's pompous brother-in-law, Jay Taylor, for instance, may be evasive at the mention of Heather Landi's name, but he is hardly the type to endanger his daughter's life. Similarly, Alex Carbine, who is dating Lacey's widowed mother, Mona, could have discovered and betrayed Lacey's hiding place, but his relationship with Mona is well established when Lacey's ordeal unexpectedly begins. He is probably not, in other words, wooing Mona to get to Lacey.

The character whose name probably would not even register on the suspect list is the criminal, Steve Abbott, and that omission accounts for the murder mystery's failure to satisfy. Abbott, Jimmy Landi's right-hand man, appears infrequently in the novel and seldom earns more than a brief mention when he does. In the novel's denouement, the final unraveling of the plot strands, Clark reveals Abbott's secret life as a drug dealer, racketeer, and thief, but because readers have seen no evidence of it, the information seems unconvincing as a motive for Heather's murder. Instead it seems a convenient ploy by which to conclude the novel. Clark fails to develop the relationship between Abbott and Jimmy Landi, for whom the younger man is almost a "surrogate son" (204); she fails to explore the slight hint of jealousy and frustration in Abbott's relationship with Jimmy that may have given his pursuit of Heather a sinister edge of personal vendetta. She also fails to examine any of the possibilities that might have provided Abbott with a convincing motive for murder. Abbott's unveiling as the novel's ultimate criminal thus gives the mystery an unearned conclusion and deprives readers of the potential satisfaction of solving the crime on their own.

As a suspense story, *Pretend You Don't See Her* lacks one of Clark's standard strategies for creating and maintaining suspense, a time constraint, and thus the novel seems rather flat. Lacey witnesses Isabelle's murder the first week of September, and she bolts for New York in late February, not because a significant date or anniversary compels her to act, but simply because Sandy Savarano has discovered her safe haven. Clark has tried to manufacture a deadline: To pacify Bonnie, who is suffering from depression following her gunshot wound and her beloved aunt's disappearance, Jay Taylor promises that Lacey will return to celebrate his daughter's fifth birthday on 1 March. Lacey, however, is unaware of this promise, so the date lacks any significance so far as her decisions are concerned. It does not, in other words, generate any real tension in the plot, becoming instead merely a convenient date by which to mark time. Lacey's situation could have continued indefinitely, but a novel, of course, must come to an end. So Clark does what she must.

It is as a mystery of identity, however, that *Pretend You Don't See Her* is least satisfying, perhaps because the novel has simply too much plot. To develop fully what are essentially thematic issues, Clark must focus on character. She must place Lacey's struggle to salvage herself from the pressure to forge a new identity at the center of her novel. Yet the novel's murder mystery, as well as the demands of suspense, makes different claims on the plot. Granted, Clark attempts to explore the thematic issues, as I will explain later in this chapter, but the novel has so much plot that she really fails to do justice to them. The novel's action moves from New York to Minnesota, with side trips to Connecticut and New Jersey, so many times that the pace seldom gives pause for reflection. Moreover, the novel's large cast of characters, including Lacey's family, who are also affected by her disappearance, requires that Clark provide sufficient details about each to put flesh on their skeletons, to give them, in other words, a reality. In consequence, Lacey's struggle to keep hold of her sense of self frequently becomes secondary to her mother's worry about her safety, the marital discord of the Parker family, Heather Landi's fear of disappointing her father and thereby incurring his wrath, and countless other details that give substance to the minor characters but divert attention from the major character. Clark's mystery of identity is in effect rather underdeveloped.

CHARACTER DEVELOPMENT

That mystery of identity is linked, of course, to Lacey Farrell, the protagonist, or central character, of *Pretend You Don't See Her*. The thirty-year-old realtor for one of Manhattan's top agencies, Parker and Parker, brings to her job a love of the city, instilled by her father, the musician Jack Farrell, and a genuine understanding of and desire to fulfill her clients' needs, qualities that have made her highly successful in a competitive field. In her quest for success, Lacey has clearly not forgotten that people matter more than money. Indeed, her relationships with her family as well as with Isabelle Waring reveal her distinguishing character traits and clarify her defining values.

A loving and loved daughter, sister, and aunt, Lacey certainly values family. In fact, she is almost unique among Clark's typical heroines in that she is "aware that [her] biological clock is ticking" (14). While she does not fret about her single status, she clearly enjoys children, especially her nephews and niece, with whom she frequently shares what they call their "Jack Farrell days" exploring the wonders of Manhattan (15), and hopes one day to be a mother herself. Frequent visits with and telephone conversations between Lacey and both her mother and her sister, Kit, reveal the genuine warmth, care, and concern in their relationships. While Kit may favor their mother in both her appearance and her tastes and Lacey may have inherited their father's "Irish coloring" (7) as well as his sensibility, any trace of sibling rivalry is clearly missing between them. In fact, Kit is Lacey's trusted confidant. In the midst of her ordeal, Lacey will even risk telephoning her sister to learn her views about the mystery and to enlist her help (268). To spare her mother some worry, Lacey will also reveal her witness protection location to her. Lacey's family connections help to define her sense of self, so she will experience their absence as a constant ache during her Alice Carroll existence.

While Lacey's relationship with Isabelle Waring certainly exceeds professional boundaries, it seems utterly typical of a sensitive and compassionate woman. When Lacey first meets Isabelle to view Heather's apartment, she understands this mother's grief and responds to it by covering Isabelle's hand with her own, a gesture that speaks instinctively of shared human suffering (13). In the weeks that follow, Isabelle, who finds "something in [Lacey's] smile and manner" that revives a "positive memory" of her daughter (9), begins to telephone the realtor daily, often to urge her to come by the apartment, sometimes to share a glass of wine or a meal, especially at twilight, what she calls the "lonesome time of the day" (22). Lacey, who still grieves her beloved father's death, responds at first to her client's personal need because she is by nature compassionate and caring. Eventually, however, she responds because Isabelle is someone she genuinely likes, someone she considers a friend (22).

Lacey's promise to fulfill Isabelle's dying request is, then, an obligation to which the young woman feels utterly committed, and that fact says much about Lacey's character as well. She is the kind of person who honors her word no matter the cost. When she removes Heather's journal from Isabelle's apartment, Lacey risks criminal prosecution for withholding evidence, but she will not renege on her promise. Instead, she finds a way to meet her obligation to Isabelle and to comply with the law. Later, when her promise to Isabelle threatens her very life, Lacey refuses to be deterred from her efforts to pursue the truth about Heather's death. Her word is her bond. To betray it would be to betray her very sense of herself.

THEMATIC ISSUES

Lacey's five-month stint in the Federal Witness Protection Program certainly tests her strong sense of self, challenging the very concept of identity, and thus it dramatizes the central theme of *Pretend You Don't See Her*. When Lacey is compelled by circumstances (and against her better judgment) to deny her past and to abandon the life that she had created for herself, she experiences a sort of dissociation of self that threatens to destroy her. Lacey does indeed have the strength of character to do what she must, especially after her beloved niece takes a bullet intended for her and she must reluctantly acknowledge that to stay in Manhattan would selfishly endanger others. But she is certainly not prepared for the intense loneliness, the paralyzing fear, and the impotent anger and frustration that become the defining characteristics of her life as Alice Carroll. As Lacey, she had earned a comfortable salary; as Alice, she is reduced to begging for cash advances from her government minder, George Svenson, to establish a meagre existence. As Lacey, she enjoyed a satisfying independence; as Alice, she seldom knows the ease of security, for even a stranger who chooses a seat behind hers in a half empty movie theatre can cause her to flee for her life (180–81). As Alice, Lacey realizes, she can never be herself because she must sacrifice one of her defining traits—her honesty.

As Alice Carroll, Lacey must, for instance, conceal her natural talent for matching people and properties when she takes a job as receptionist at a small realty office. She must also withhold information from those who would befriend her, including Tom Lynch, a man who, under other circumstances, she could easily let herself love. Because she must build every shred of her new life on lies, Lacey feels herself disappearing, and this loss of identity deeply troubles her. Tom, for instance, may be attracted to Alice, but "he likes someone who doesn't really exist, [she thinks] with a trace of bitterness" (151). Yet for all intents and purposes, neither does Lacey. Rather like her namesake Alice, the imaginary creation of the English novelist Lewis Carroll, who shrinks in size when she falls through the hole into the strange and bewildering world of Wonderland, Lacey begins to contract when she lands in the strange and bewildering world of Minneapolis. Carroll's Alice, however, at least retained her name during her adventures. Lacey, in contrast, must even renounce that symbolic mark of identity as she lives what becomes her nightmare. So frustrated and uncertain does Clark's heroine eventually become that at one point she wants nothing more than that George Svenson should confirm her identity by using her real name: *"Please, just once, call me Lacey,"* she wants to shout (209).

To reclaim her identity, Lacey must ultimately leave the Federal Witness Protection Program, for it is impossible to live as an impostor. Certainly her decision is risky. Physical danger, however, pales in comparison, Clark makes clear, to the psychological disorder that results from the loss of one's essential sense of self. Confronting the nightmare, moreover, is both liberating and empowering. It releases Lacey, for instance, who wants so much to be a "truthful" person again (168), from the tissue of lies that has become her life and reinforces the very habits of mind and being by which others have known her and, most important, by which she has defined herself. When, at the end of the novel, she asserts to Tom, "Alice doesn't live here anymore" and claims her name, that sign of the self (305), Lacey has indeed achieved a great victory. It is impossible, Clark makes clear, to "pretend you don't see" someone who knows she exists.

"Trapped in a lie" (219), Lacey experiences a crisis of identity. Hers, of course, is one of the consequences of deception, and as such, it raises a secondary theme of *Pretend You Don't See Her*. Throughout the novel, Clark makes clear through Lacey's example that deception undermines the sense of self. Through her subplot about Nick Mars, the corrupt police-man, she makes clear that it compromises institutions as well. When Heather Landi's journal goes missing from Detective Ed Sloane's locked private cubby, he is sickened to think that one of his trusted colleagues could be the thief, yet it is a strong possibility. The policeman has a habit of leaving his keys in the pocket of his coat, which he usually drapes over his desk chair. Anyone in the precinct could have lifted his keys and stolen the journal, but probably nobody from the outside could have done so. Nevertheless, Ed is dumbfounded when he watches the videotape that has recorded his partner's theft of the keys during a subsequent set-up designed to catch the culprit. Mars's grandfather and father had been police officers, so this third-generation legacy had "been given every break" in his own career. "Why?" Sloane can only wonder (271), a question to which he must definitely want an answer when he eventually witnesses Mars's attempt to murder Savarano and thereby eliminate any-one who could testify against him and the drug cartel for which he works (299).

The price of deception in this case is both personal and institutional. From the moment Ed Sloane realizes that his partner is bent, for instance, it takes all his self-control to continue working with Mars (286), especially when what he wants most is "ten minutes alone with the jerk" (272). Unable to trust the person who is supposed to protect his back, Sloane feels not only betrayed but also vulnerable. Mars's deception has also sullied his reputation as well as the precinct's. In consequence, U.S. At-torney Gary Baldwin feels justified in withholding information from Sloane and his colleagues and taunts them about their professional short-comings (159–60). Jimmy Landi hires a private investigator to pursue his daughter's murder case (144), and Lacey determines to keep her own counsel and eventually to abandon police protection altogether. After all, authorities are clearly incapable of safeguarding her. Police corruption, Clark's example indicates, strikes at the very heart of the institution that it represents and compromises, perhaps irrevocably, the public trust. To reinforce her thematic point, Clark includes "one of Nick Mars's little witticisms," the observation that the initials of the Long Island Express-way spell the word "LIE" (287). Nick chuckles at his own cleverness, but clearly deceit is very serious business, with consequences that always matter.

The third thematic issue of *Pretend You Don't See Her* continues Clark's recurring examination of the legacy of grief. Lacey, for instance, has never quite recovered from the shock of her beloved father's sudden death shortly after she had graduated from college (8). As much as she loves her mother, she misses the man from whom she inherited her love of the city and who had taught her to sing a repertoire of Broadway show tunes. Despite the intervening years since her father's death, Lacey still grieves his absence from her life and even finds her friendship with Isabelle War-ing difficult at times because "sharing her pain" (22) rubs open Lacey's old wound. In moments of stress, however, Lacey conjures up an image of her father that gives her strength. His *"protective spirit,"* for instance, seemed to have urged her to slam shut and then bolt the door against Isabelle's killer, thereby saving her own life (29). Months later, when she is trying to erase Tom Lynch's memory from her heart and mind, she evokes the image of her father, who chides her for failing to face her real feelings (208–09). Grief, then, is only part of Lacey's response to her father's death. At some level, in fact, she has learned to be comfortable with his spiritual presence in her life.

For Isabelle Waring and Jimmy Landi, however, grief is still too raw to give them any ease. Isabelle, of course, makes no effort to conceal the devastation of her daughter's loss, so her refusal to accept the official verdict of accidental death is distressing to Jimmy. He considers her belief that Heather was murdered the obsessive need of a woman who cannot let go rather than a probable explanation for their daughter's death and scoffs at his former wife's efforts to investigate a case that is not a case. Yet Jimmy has his own unresolved feelings about Heather's death. He, too, cannot "let go of the constant need for his daughter's presence" (17), and he still takes comfort from his sense that she watches him—as indeed she does. The walls of his popular Manhattan restaurant are decorated with murals on which images of Heather at various stages in her life had been painted. Although Jimmy finds these images disturbing now (17), neither can he order them removed from the colorful Venetian scenes. Only Isabelle's murder will compel this sad man who hides his grief behind a gruff exterior to follow his own advice to his former wife to move forward in life and banish Heather's image from his daily sight. As painful as moving forward may be, Clark's novel suggests, it is finally necessary. It is what the living do.

In a novel crowded with thematic issues, Clark raises a fourth in her exploration of the parent-child relationship, a theme on which she had previously focused, particularly in *While My Pretty One Sleeps* (1989), *I'll Be Seeing You* (1993), and *Remember Me* (1994). Lacey is again a starting point for Clark's development of this theme. Her warm and loving relationship with her father had, after all, laid the foundation for her character, interests, and sensibility, and her equally supportive mother continues to be a source of strength and stability in her life. Two other parent-child relationships in *Pretend You Don't See Her*, however, make clear the damage parents can do their children, however inadvertently. Together, the three examples provide evidence of the power and complexity of that life-giving and life-sustaining bond.

Like Lacey, Heather Landi appears to have had a supportive and satisfying relationship with both of her parents despite the divorce that had shuttled her between two households. Both had doted on their only child, born ten years into their marriage and after Isabelle had suffered three miscarriages (11). Both had encouraged her talents and dreams. But Heather's journal exposes another side of her relationship with her parents, particularly with her father. Heather so feared disappointing him that she led a secret life, and the price of her inability to be honest with her father may have been her life. In the days before her death, Heather wrote repeatedly about being "trapped" between two immovable obstacles and of "her worries about hurting" her father (275). It bothers Jimmy terribly that Heather feared him so much that she would not confide in him (261), and, Clark's novel suggests, it should disturb him.

Jimmy's love was a good deal about control. That need, in fact, had driven Isabelle from him (11). Jimmy may have generously purchased a Manhattan apartment for his talented daughter, but it was his choice, not hers. In fact, she had already signed the papers on a West Side co-op when Jimmy informed her that he had purchased for her a luxury apartment on the East Side in a building complete with a doorman to ensure her safety (12). Fearful of incurring her father's anger by telling him about her purchase, Heather had instead been willing to trade sexual favors for Rick Parker's promise to tear up her original contract (234–35). Such desperation about an apartment puts in perspective Heather's secret relationship with Steve Abbott. If her father would not approve her choice of something so seemingly inconsequential as an apartment, she could be certain that he would never permit her to love the sophisticated older man, no matter his own relationship with her father and especially in light of the information that Max Hoffman, Jimmy's trusted employee, threatened to reveal about him.

No matter how much Jimmy loved his daughter, he was not willing to permit her to be independent, to grow and learn even from mistakes, but parents must do exactly that if their children are to develop into responsible and productive adults. Jimmy effectively prevented Heather from having a life of her own and from developing an adult relationship with him. Had she had that relationship, she may have been able to confide in her father, and he may have been able not to idolize her, to adore her ideal image, the evidence of which was painted on his restaurant walls, but to accept her full humanity, including her flaws and weaknesses. Both their lives might have been enriched for it.

Jimmy's failure to give Heather the freedom she clearly wanted to shape her own life was as destructive in its way as Richard Parker's indulgence of his son Rick's every whim. "Given everything that money could buy" (201), Rick received a Mercedes convertible for his seventeenth birthday and a Central Park West apartment to mark his college graduation (200), but what he most needed—boundaries that would teach discipline, an example that would instill morals—money could not buy. Richard Parker, moreover, did not even try to give them to his son. Instead, he paid the damages when Rick trashed a fraternity house during a "wild party" (199) and settled out of court a sexual assault complaint that a secretary filed against his son (200). He even dressed "his mistress of the month," his wife tells police, in a maid's uniform to bring her into the family home (232). Parker, according to his wife, had "taught [his son] to think of himself as above any discipline, or even any sense of decency" (231–32). In spoiling his child, he had destroyed his "goodness and promise" (231), and Rick had fulfilled his expectations. He had become a ne'er-do-well, prone to drunken carousing and addicted to cocaine, a thirty-one-year-old boy who had never been made to accept responsibility or exercise self-control. Only when his mother finally masters her own fear of her husband and secrets her son to a drug rehabilitation center does it seem that Rick Parker may have a chance to become an adult. His chastened demeanor as he relates to police the sad and sordid tale of his relationship with Heather Landi certainly suggests that Priscilla Parker's faith in her son may not have been misplaced.

Clark's exploration of the parent-child relationship makes clear that it is crucial to the development of a sense of self, and as such, it extends her examination of the theme of identity. From their parents, children learn life lessons. They absorb values and attitudes that will be with them into adulthood. From their parents, they learn as well, and perhaps more importantly, their own value. Lacey's parents loved and nurtured but also respected their daughter. Even during her childhood, she and her father were "pals" (7), a term that signifies a special relationship among equals. From such a childhood, Lacey develops the strong sense of self that will see her through her "Alice Carroll" ordeal. Neither Heather Landi nor Rick Parker, in contrast, ever really becomes an independent adult, chiefly because their powerful fathers would not relinquish control. Their value, such control may have suggested to them, lay not in themselves but in their relationship to their fathers. Heather was an ideal, Rick a second self. Neither ever really achieved a separate, self-asserted identity, and that was and is, perhaps, the real tragedy of their lives.

A FEMINIST READING OF *PRETEND YOU DON'T SEE HER*

The powerful men in *Pretend You Don't See Her* certainly raise some issues about the nature of patriarchal, or male-dominated, society, and thus they provide Clark with an opportunity to engage in some rather insightful cultural criticism. Such a critique is based on feminist literary theory and concerns itself primarily with issues of power and gender. It focuses, in other words, on issues of control, especially, but not exclusively, as they limit a woman's sense of power and authority over her own existence. Because feminism investigates the realm of literature as well as sociological, economic, and political ideas, it invites readers to consider the ways in which gender issues are reflected in the text, especially if we view the world of the novel as a representation or recreation of its society. From such a perspective, the powerful men and the institutions they create in *Pretend You Don't See Her* certainly seem destructive of human potential.

To place such a critique in perspective, we need first to have a basic understanding of the theory that grounds it. Histories of feminist criticism generally divide it into three broad phases and stances. The first phase involves analysis of patriarchal culture, a term for the institutions, attitudes, and beliefs of a society dominated by men. Feminist critics thus analyze literary interpretations of male-dominated society to expose what Elaine Showalter calls "the misogyny of literary practice," the stereotypical images of women in literature, "the literary abuse or textual harassment of women in classics and popular male literature, and [the] exclusion of women from literary history" (5). In the second phase, feminist critics set out to map the territory of the female imagination. Concerned with women as writers giving expression to the female experience through their work, feminist critics seek to define the distinctive means of communication and the subjects and concerns that distinguish women's texts from men's. These critics generally share the idea that gender difference determines much about a person's life experience and hence about one's means of communicating, reading, or writing. Feminist criticism of the third phase focuses on the shared experience of all people rather than the fundamental differences between men and women, emphasizing the humanity of all people regardless of gender as the foundation of real equality and understanding among people.

Whatever their stance, feminist critics do seem to share one important idea about literary criticism: the impossibility of achieving objectivity. For years, critics believed that the author's personal history, the social expectations of his or her time, and the historical events that occurred during the author's life had no bearing on understanding literary works. Instead, literature was a world of its own, complete in itself, and thus could be evaluated without reference to personal, social, and historical contexts. Feminist critics believe that such objectivity is impossible. Instead, they acknowledge and promote subjectivity—responses based on experience and belief. They recognize that every reader brings both elements to the literary work and thus understands literature from a personal perspective.

In Clark's novel, patriarchy is chiefly associated with the world of business, where competition is the game, and embodied in two figures, Jimmy Landi and Richard Parker, experts at playing and winning. Both have created successful businesses, Landi in food and entertainment, including casinos, and Parker in real estate. Both maintain a firm hand on their empires, delegating daily operations to employees but retaining all financial control for themselves. Both also bring attitudes about power and prerogative into their personal lives, where they dominate their families' lives, as if taking seriously the old adage that "a man's home is his castle." Accustomed to wielding absolute power, neither Landi nor Parker tolerates disobedience, which explains both Heather's and Rick's fear of their fathers. It also puts in perspective Isabelle Waring's decision to divorce Landi and Priscilla Parker's cowardice after years of infidelity and cruel bullying (111).

Competition may be the game in the business world, but it clearly breeds some destructive attitudes and behaviors that have serious consequences on human life. The Landi and Parker families certainly become victims of male power and prerogative and thus illustrate the dangers of patriarchy. The example of Steve Abbott offers a provocative elaboration of the point. Because he is the novel's true villain, it seems impossible that he could be a victim. In the context of a cultural and feminist critique, however, he certainly is, for the attitudes and behaviors that lead to business success breed the Steve Abbotts of the world as well.

Abbott is clearly ambitious, a quality much valued in the competitive world of business. He wants to be more than Jimmy's right-hand man, and as his "surrogate son" (204), he expects to be. Yet Jimmy never fails to remind him that he is the "boss" (52; 110), and Abbott, who, he tells Jimmy, has just celebrated his forty-fifth birthday, must surely feel his opportunities passing. Jimmy's desire "to rub another success in everyone's face" (102) may not have included Abbott's, but it must certainly have fanned the flames of resentment that the debonair man skillfully conceals. Ambitious, competitive, ruthless, Abbott has all the qualities that have resulted in success for Jimmy Landi. Indeed, he dropped out of Cornell University to develop them under Landi's tutelage (18). So he is in many ways the epitome of the ethic he has embraced, an extreme example of the man with the competitive edge to succeed, which is, after all, what counts.

This competitive ethic is clearly male-defined and thus extends into other male-dominated institutions, chiefly law enforcement, in *Pretend You Don't See Her*. Rather than work cooperatively to apprehend Isabelle Waring's murderer, U.S. Attorney Gary Baldwin and Detective Ed Sloane and the rival bodies that each represents engage in an unprofessional and what amounts to a reckless game of one-upmanship. They withhold information from each other and taunt each other like schoolboys about any mistake or weakness. After Heather's journal, for instance, disappears from his locked cubby and Baldwin berates him for the theft, Sloane determines that he will be the one to bring Rick Parker in for questioning. After all, Baldwin had failed to tell him that federal agents had information linking the realtor to Heather Landi (198–99). And Sloane makes certain that he, rather than Baldwin, apprehends Savarano and rescues Lacey when his lone action, especially given the fact that the rogue cop Nick Mars accompanies him, could have ended disastrously. In law enforcement and other public institutions, there should not be petty rivalries and competing jurisdictions, for everyone is striving for the same goal. But law enforcement is a traditional bastion of male power and privilege, so the male-identified ethic of competition rather than the female-identified ethic of cooperation prevails. Left unsaid is the point that cooperation might have achieved the same results in less time and without unnecessarily endangering innocent lives.

By placing Lacey within the competitive world of real estate and even making her an employee of Parker and Parker, Clark ensures that the ethic she describes is in fact male-identified. Lacey, after all, succeeds in the business environment, but the virus of ruthless competition does not infect her. She sells property because she does her "homework on a prospective listing" (8), develops relationships with the workers in the various buildings that the agency handles so that they are willing to assist her, and learns about her clients' needs and desires. In fact, she takes as much pride in and pleasure from matching a client to a property as she takes enjoyment from haggling about price (140). Lacey's personal approach to the business world is female-identified, based on relationship, cooperation, and consensus, qualities that are traditionally associated with women. As such, it provides an alternative model for success. Indeed, it challenges that male-identified ethic that clearly has the potential not only to hurt others and to undermine institutions, but also to damage the self. From a feminist perspective, a patriarchal culture ultimately is an equal opportunity menace, harming both men and women with its insistence on power, prerogative, and control.

In the end, *Pretend You Don't See Her* raises a number of provocative issues, too many, perhaps, to do justice to them all. The novel may simply have too much plot, too little character, too much mystery, too little suspense to satisfy all the demands of the genre. But in Lacey Farrell, Clark gives readers an engaging and a sympathetic heroine who meets every challenge with courage and resolve, a heroine who certainly has the capability of supporting the novel's central ideas. Lacey's refusal to be anyone but herself is, in fact, testament to everything positive in and necessary to Clark's worldview.

You Belong to Me
(1998)

Mary Higgins Clark's fifteenth best-selling novel of mystery and suspense, *You Belong to Me*, is another cautionary tale of sexual predators that glances back to 1991's *Loves Music, Loves to Dance* for its contemporary subject. In that previous work, young women looking for love through the personal dating ads become the unwitting victims of a ruthless serial killer determined to avenge the pain of rejection. In *You Belong to Me*, Clark modifies details of plot: Here, a serial killer intent on making women pay for the predatory behavior of the stepmother who cheated him of his inheritance targets lonely women enjoying luxury cruises. But her focus remains essentially the same. Both novels explore the consequences of modern society for independent women who live on their own terms. The subject thus allows Clark to extend her examination of the changing face of contemporary society. It allows her as well to continue to explore some truths of the human heart and mind, for in *You Belong to Me*, loneliness and grief, jealousy and revenge, legacies of the personal past, prove powerful psychological forces that shape human behavior. Like *Loves Music, Loves to Dance*, *You Belong to Me* thus demonstrates Clark's ability to extend the boundaries of her genre.

You Belong to Me focuses on Dr. Susan Chandler, a clinical psychologist who hosts a popular radio talk show, *Ask Dr. Susan*. When she interviews Dr. Donald Richards, the author of a book entitled *Vanishing Women*, for a program about women who disappear, she unwittingly becomes the target of a devious serial killer. During the program, Susan focuses on the mysterious and still unsolved disappearance of a wealthy investment advisor and CNBC stock research analyst, Regina Clausen, who had disembarked from a world cruise in Hong Kong three years before and vanished without a trace. When one of her audience telephones with information that could link a turquoise ring engraved with the phrase "You belong to me" that an attractive man had once given her on a luxury cruise to Regina's disappearance, Susan determines to pursue the lead, especially after the caller, Carolyn Wells, is pushed beneath the wheels of a delivery van from a crowded Manhattan sidewalk. As Susan's search intensifies and she discovers the connection between Carolyn Wells and Regina Clausen, she realizes as well that the killer not only stalks lonely women on cruise ships but also is eliminating anyone who might possibly expose his identity. Even more frightening, she begins to fear that the killer may be one of the men in her life and that she, in fact, may be marked for murder.

PLOT

Clark begins *You Belong to Me* with a brief prologue that takes readers inside the mind of a killer, a narrative strategy that she uses frequently to establish a mood of tense horror. From the killer's perspective, readers watch his cool detachment as he stalks his victim, Regina Clausen, and note the pleasure he takes in the "thrill" (11) of the kill. As he surveys her appearance, concluding that "she could have been quite attractive if she only knew . . . how to present herself," and then offers a "silent toast" (12) as he mentally takes possession of her, the killer exposes both his twisted mind and murderous plan to readers, who are powerless, like the victim, because they cannot act on their knowledge. In the prologue, Clark wastes no time building up to murder because nothing is more horrifying than murder itself. She simply plunges readers into the nightmare, a strategy that is also calculated to hook them to her plot.

The contemporary action of *You Belong to Me* begins three years later, with Susan Chandler's radio talk show interview with Donald Richards. Events spiral quickly out of Susan's control. One potential source of information, Carolyn Wells, soon lies in the hospital in a coma, the victim of a traffic "accident." Another, the waitress Tiffany Smith, who had promised to let Susan examine the turquoise ring engraved with "You belong to me" that a boyfriend had purchased for her from a souvenir shop in Greenwich Village, is stabbed to death in a parking lot. A third, the Indian craftsman of the turquoise rings, Abdul Parki, is knifed in his shop. Even eighty-year-old Hilda Johnson, a witness who insists that Carolyn did not fall but was pushed under the wheels of the delivery van, becomes the target of a killer determined not only to avoid detection, but also to complete his "mission" (19) to murder five lonely women.

That mission acts as a narrative strategy to raise the novel's suspense by providing the time constraint that Clark believes necessary to her effect. The killer has already murdered four women, readers learn early in the novel, and, now alerted to Susan's inquiry, has begun to trawl for his last victim. If Susan fails to unmask the killer, he stands every chance of outwitting authorities and escaping detection forever. After all, he has already managed to kill seven in what appear to be random incidents. What makes Susan's efforts even more crucial is the killer's identification of his final victim—Dee Chandler Harriman. If Susan does not find the connection between the turquoise rings and Regina Clausen's death, then her sister seems destined to disappear during a two-week cruise through the Panama Canal. Her mission, in other words, has suddenly become personal, but she does not even know it. Time is now a key element to Clark's plot, not least because readers know that the killer intends to murder Susan, too.

The title of Clark's novel also serves as a crucial plot element, for the lyrics of the song with which it shares its name, "You Belong to Me," provide clues to the killer's own plot to avenge his stepmother's treachery. When Virginia Owen met Alexander Wright's father on an ocean cruise, she liked to sing the song into his ear as they danced in the moonlight. After the widower, who was thirty-five years older than the attractive woman, married Virginia, they spent their honeymoon following the lyrics of the song, beginning in Egypt, where they could *See the pyramids along the Nile.* Years later, Clark's killer stalks his first victim, who disappears while in Egypt, on a cruise to the Middle East. Regina Clausen, who disappeared after her cruise ship had docked in Bali, may have been unlucky enough to *Watch the sunrise on a tropic isle* with him, while Carolyn Wells may have avoided her fate when she failed to *See the marketplace in old Algiers* with the man who gave her a turquoise ring on her ocean cruise (although she nearly meets it on a Manhattan street). When Susan begins to wonder if a different woman had disappeared in Algiers and if another had met the killer when she "[*Flew*] *the ocean in a silver plane*," she has finally found the connection between seemingly unrelated events. The crucial question, of course, is whether she can unmask a killer before he and another victim *See the jungle when it's wet with rain.*

Clark frequently uses song titles to provide some insight into her novels' themes and concerns, but in *You Belong to Me* the song itself clearly has an important plot function, a fact that differentiates her use of this strategy and indeed this work from others in her canon.

POINT OF VIEW

From the novel's opening, it is also clear that Clark intends to deviate from her usual third-person omniscient point of view in *You Belong to Me*. Not only does Clark begin her novel from the killer's perspective, or from a first-person point of view, but she also intersperses that perspective throughout the novel. Its effect is chilling, and thus the narrative strategy enhances the novel's suspense. Because readers know his murderous plot, they understand his devious mind and twisted logic. They understand his cleverness as well. Here is a man who can systematically kill as well as avoid detection. Nothing, it seems, can stop him.

Yet as the novel's events unfold, readers also realize that the killer is becoming unnerved by Susan's probing. After knifing Hilda Johnson, for instance, he worries that her dying words may have placed a curse on him and has the eerie sensation that his right foot, onto which Hilda's hand had fallen at her death, grows "heavier and heavier. It felt almost as if [her] thick-fingered hand were still lying on it" (67), he thinks with a bit of panic that betrays some psychological disquiet. After his attack on Carolyn Wells, he sleeps "fitfully" (74), waking throughout the night to watch television news bulletins in hopes of learning about her condition. Clark's use of the first-person point of view gives readers direct insight into an increasingly more desperate and thus more dangerous criminal. Had she narrated the tale from an omniscient, or all-knowing, and detached point of view, readers would have had far less understanding of the killer's state of mind. Clark, however, clearly wanted them to have that knowledge, which essentially makes *You Belong to Me* a tale of psychological suspense. The source of its horror lies in the minds of both the criminal and the reader, for their own imaginings create the tension that constitutes suspense.

CHARACTER DEVELOPMENT

Susan Chandler, *You Belong to Me*'s central character, is a typical Clark heroine. An accomplished professional woman in her early thirties, she is intelligent, resourceful, and fearless in her determination. Compassionate and caring, she is sensitive to others' needs, and not simply because she is a psychologist. She understands Jane Clausen's unremitting grief for her missing daughter, for instance, and recognizes the loneliness and vulnerability in Tiffany Smith's voice when the wistful waitress telephones her radio talk show with information about the turquoise ring. What Susan is perhaps less aware of, however, or at least less willing to admit, is her own vulnerability, for as is typical of Clark's heroines, she nurses a previous hurt that continues to affect her life.

Betrayal is the source of Susan's pain. Her parents' bitter divorce after nearly forty years of marriage has left Susan caught between her unhappy mother and her happily remarried father and has called into question her cherished version of her idyllic family life (168). She may be an adult child with a life independent of her parents' lives, but their divorce has left her feeling disconcertingly abandoned. Now she has begun to admit the fissures that had always been part of her family life—her father's insecurities, for instance, and her sister's jealousy. Admitting them, however, does not necessarily make them easy to bear, and some are more difficult than others with which to live.

Most troubling for Susan is her relationship with her sister Dee. Ten years before, Susan had been in love with and been loved by Jack, a professional photographer, and then her big sister, a top fashion model, had claimed him for her own. Susan still dreams of the betrayal, and "it [bothers] her deeply that after all these years, a dream . . . [can] bring all the memories flooding back" (68). Susan knows that had she been in Dee's position, had she been attracted to the man her sister loved, she would have acted honorably. She would never have allowed jealousy to blind her to the right course. So while she may still love her sister, she cannot truly trust her—and Dee has given her new reason to doubt. Just as Susan is beginning a relationship with Alex Wright, Dee begins her own pursuit of the attractive and eligible bachelor, reopening old wounds that reveal the psychologist's own vulnerabilities. Despite her appearance of self-confidence, Susan is thus rather like all of the novel's vulnerable women. Professional success does not exempt her from private doubts and personal pain.

Dee Chandler Harriman, Susan's elder sister, is a study in loneliness and insecurity of the sort that made victims of Regina Clausen as well as her "sisters in death" (85), Veronica, Constance, and Monica. As such, she plays an important thematic role in *You Belong to Me*. A former top fashion model who now runs her own agency, Dee, who is "thankful" to have her high school diploma and resents the fact that her parents had not "insisted" that she go to college (47), understands that she has succeeded on the basis of her appearance rather than her intelligence, on extrinsic rather than intrinsic qualities, in other words. Thus, she feels inferior to her younger sister, who trained as a lawyer as well as a psychologist. Even something as simple as scrambling an egg elicits both self-pity and jealous pique from the unhappy woman. "That's another thing Susan is better at than I am," she thinks when she burns her dinner. "She's a good cook" (103). Feeling as she does, Dee, who is still grieving her husband's accidental death two years before and "[misses] being married" (47), easily justifies her efforts to snare Alex Wright from Susan. Dee is also tailor-made to become the victim of a man who preys on lonely and insecure women. Like his other victims, she is susceptible to male attention because it boosts her fragile sense of self and gives hope that she is worthy of love.

Dee is not, of course, the only woman plagued by self-doubt in *You Belong to Me*. Perhaps rather surprisingly, however, given male stereotypes of strength and confidence, nearly all of Clark's male characters are as insecure as the women. Justin Wells, for instance, has lived in fear all his life that someday he would be exposed as the failure he believes himself to be. Despite a career as an "outstanding college football player" and his partnership in an architectural firm, he begins every new project "with the agonizing certainty that *this* was the one he would flub" (40). Plagued by self-doubts and fearing failure, he is also convinced that his wife, Carolyn, will inevitably leave him (41). Two years before, when Carolyn escaped on an ocean cruise, his intense jealousy and distrust of her nearly made his worst fear come true.

Susan's father, Charles Chandler, is another example of the novel's insecure males. A self-made success, he is "still in awe of important people" (54) and fearful that he may betray his humble beginnings. His marriage to Susan's mother had transformed him. She had taught him all the "social graces" and had encouraged him to leave the family business to develop his own. "She gave him the self-confidence to succeed," Susan sadly muses, "then he took hers away" (43). Just before their fortieth wedding anniversary, he had walked out on his marriage, perhaps to leave behind his past, perhaps to reassure himself that he was still desirable, for he had dyed his gray hair, married a woman called Binky, and built a "palatial home" (14) within no time. Now, as if to deny his age, he insists that his daughter call him "Charles" (15) rather than "Dad." Susan, who is saddened by her parents' immaturity (14), wishes that her father "didn't need to pretend" (55) that he is someone other than himself.

The attractive philanthropist Alexander Wright is also a study in insecurity. With the "authority and poise that were the product of generations of breeding" (61), he still strikes Susan as "shy," a quality that she finds intriguing about him (61). An only child and "the product of a late marriage" (61), Alex had been raised by hard parents, neither of whom provided much affection or approval. In fact, Jim Curley, Alex's chauffeur, recalls that Alex's mother, who would "bite your head off for nothing," was "always on Alex when he was a kid" (60) and finds it "a miracle he turned out so fine" (60). Alex, however, did not turn out as fine as Curley thinks. In fact, his deprived childhood had made him a "loner" (303) in school and eventually an embittered adult. As chairman of the Wright Foundation, he resents signing every check that dispenses the fortune that should be his. Had his parents been different sorts, his biography suggests, Alex might have felt worthy. He might have been happy with himself. He might not have become a ruthless serial killer.

THEMATIC DEVELOPMENT

Clark fills *You Belong to Me* with a cast of insecure characters both male and female to advance at least in part one of the novel's central themes—the powerful presence of the past in human life. Susan and Dee, Justin and Alex, indeed all of the characters in Clark's novel, have been shaped by their past, and thus it continues to exert its influence on their present. Clark's novel makes clear, however, that only by exploring the territory that lies deep within the heart and mind can the individual come to self-knowledge and self-worth and that such exploration is therefore essential. Justin will certainly lose Carolyn if he cannot master his doubts and fears, and the Chandler sisters will always have a troubled relationship so long as Dee remains jealous of Susan and Susan fails to admit her hurt. Facing the past, however, Clark's novel makes clear, is both empowering and liberating. Certainly her decision to make Susan Chandler a psychologist underscores this point, giving this detail of character thematic weight. The goal of the psychologist, after all, is to help the troubled chart their dark territories and in so doing conquer them. Most of Clark's characters clearly need to face their pasts and overcome their weaknesses. Otherwise they risk becoming victims of them.

A corollary to Clark's thematic exploration of the need to face the past is her emphasis on the debilitating effect of unresolved grief. Three years after her daughter Regina's disappearance from a cruise ship, Jane Clausen, for example, feels the pain of her loss as if it were only yesterday that she had learned the news. Feeling "as if she were frozen inside" (29), she knows instinctively that Regina is dead, but has constructed a comforting "fantasy" to explain her disappearance (30). Now she wants nothing more than that her own death from the debilitating illness that rages within her frail body should come soon, that she might join her daughter. Jane's grief, however, seems to have a life of its own, and it will not give her ease until Regina's killer is brought to justice. However unwilling, therefore, she is initially to cooperate with Susan Chandler's investigation into her daughter's disappearance, she finds it impossible not to assist her once Susan has unearthed a plausible connection between the turquoise ring found among Regina's personal effects and the one identical to it in Carolyn's possession.

Like Jane Clausen, Donald Richards cannot put his grief to rest, perhaps because the pain of his loss is mingled with an almost overwhelming sense of guilt. Had he not convinced his wife, Kathy, a top fashion model, to fulfill her work commitments four years before, despite her own misgivings, and go on a photo shoot in the Catskills, she might not have drowned when the canoe in which she was posing had capsized and her heavy Victorian gown had pulled her underwater. A psychiatrist and criminologist, Richards has coped with his feelings by writing a book, *Vanishing Women*, detailing the case histories of women who have disappeared, as if telling their stories will somehow mitigate his guilt. He has also packed away his remaining photos of Kathy, "hoping that it would bring some sense of closure" (44) to this chapter of his life. Neither effort, however, has been successful, and he knows that a "sense of unfinished business" (44) will continue to haunt him until the icy lake in which she drowned relinquishes her body.

Two people in similar circumstances, Jane Clausen and Donald Richards serve as living proof of the need to face the past. Irresolution hounds the mind and harries the heart. Human beings have an instinctual need to know. However painful it may be to learn the truth, it is even more painful to live with uncertainty. By the end of *You Belong to Me*, Jane Clausen has her truth. She knows the identity of Regina's killer and thus can rest in peace. Donald Richards has also begun to forgive himself for the accident that claimed his wife and to move forward with his own life. He moves to his mother's attic all his reminders of Kathy, a symbolic gesture that suggests that although she will remain attached to his life as a parent is always connected to a child, she will no longer occupy his house, his mind. Facing the past and writing his book have helped him to a measure of peace. In Jane Clausen and Donald Richards, Clark thus offers additional evidence of a recurrent theme.

You Belong to Me also has a topical theme, for like *Loves Music, Loves to Dance*, it suggests in its subject the degree to which independent women are at risk in contemporary society. As Donald Richards tells Susan, "A shy, lonely woman is particularly vulnerable when she is out of a familiar environment in which she has the reassurance and security of her job and family" (23). No matter how intelligent or accomplished, how poised or sophisticated, women who live on their own terms, Clark reiterates on her novel's final pages, "can be lured into dubious and sometimes fatal relationships by men who prey on them" (316). Such men, Clark makes clear through her example of Alex Wright, are adept at recognizing and exploiting weakness, and they understand that a woman's desire to be desired gives them power. At a stockholders' meeting or on the air for CNBC, Regina Clausen is "forceful" and self-confident, but as soon as Alex spies her "sitting wistfully and alone" in the ship's dining room and witnesses "her tremulous, almost girlish pleasure" when asked to dance (12), he marks her his next victim. She has betrayed her very human need to be loved and her fear that it will never happen, and thus she is vulnerable to his flattery and attention.

Independent women, Clark's novel makes clear, must be vigilant against male predators. They may now earn a place in the boardroom, and not merely for taking minutes. They may now wield the scalpel, and not just the thermometer. They may even command a battalion or a flight to the moon, and not just lend moral support to their husbands' efforts. Yet they deceive themselves if they believe they have the freedom and independence of men. It may be a sad truth, but it is certainly the point of Clark's cautionary tale. After all, Donald Richards has written a whole book about vanishing women, and Susan Chandler could have been among them. In the face of such evidence, it seems hard to discount Clark's point.

A NEW HISTORICIST READING OF *YOU BELONG TO ME*

To achieve their ends, authors rely upon the conventions of literature, the accepted improbabilities of narrative technique and the traditional meanings that reside in or have been attached to certain words and objects. This fact is especially true of writers of formulaic fiction such as Mary Higgins Clark. When readers open the pages of one of her novels, they expect certain events to occur and certain character types to appear. They anticipate certain responses on their part because she writes a novel of suspense, a category of fiction with identifiable conventions. The suspense novel, for instance, relies upon the threat of danger and an atmosphere of menace and the manipulation of time and event to achieve them. It relies as well upon a central character undeserving of his or her circumstances, a character about whom readers care. A suspense novel that did not conform to these conventions might very well disappoint readers for its failure to meet expectations.

Mary Higgins Clark, the acknowledged "Queen of Suspense," seldom, if ever, disappoints her readers. In fact, she delivers on a formula every time out, and that fact offers the new historicist critic reason to analyze her fiction. Although it has less obvious ideological commitments than Marxism or feminism, new historicism, a literary theory that developed in the 1980s, shares their interest in the investigation of the use and distribution of power in different cultures. Drawing on the insights of modern anthropology, new historicism attempts to isolate the fundamental values in texts and cultures, and it regards texts both as evidence of basic cultural patterns and as forces in cultural and social change.

Many of the most influential practitioners of the new historicism come out of the schools of Marxism and feminism, and like critics from those fields, they seek to uncover the ideological commitments in texts. They are also concerned about historical and cultural differences and the ways in which texts represent them. Personal commitments and specific political agendas, however, are usually less important, at least explicitly, to new historicists. In fact, feminists and new historicists, as well as Marxists and new historicists, frequently disagree about the role that personal politics should play in the practice of criticism. While some view new historicism as politically to the left in its analysis of traditional cultural values, critics on the left tend to regard new historicist assumptions as conservative.

Whatever its fundamental political commitments, however, new historicism is especially interested in social groups generally ignored by other literary historians, and it refuses to privilege "literature," or works of serious literary intention, over other printed, oral, or material texts. The new historicists also give special attention to popular literature, to the works of writers such as Mary Higgins Clark and other authors of formulaic fiction, because they believe that all texts in a culture express its values and attitudes and are thus equally useful in determining the larger belief systems of which they are a part. The new historicist thus tends to see texts as less specifically individual and distinctive than some other critics, particularly formalists, do. In fact, the primary concern of the new historicist is the prevailing tendencies shared across a culture and thus shared across all kinds of texts, whatever their literary value or political aim.

By its very nature, the novel of suspense, like similar literary genres such as the mystery, the police procedural, and the spy thriller, is conservative in nature. It is strongly on the side of law and order. "On the social level," as the literary critic and mystery writer Julian Symons explains, "crime literature [offers] to its readers . . . a reassuring world in which those who [try] to disturb the established order [are] always discovered and punished" (21). Certainly Mary Higgins Clark's novels of suspense confirm the persistence of these values. Clark's criminals, including Alexander Wright, are unambiguously evil. Readers may understand their motivation, but it does not excuse their actions. In fact, their violence against the innocent makes them deserving of the harshest punishment, which is indeed their fate.

Clark's novels of suspense suggest as well another, and surprising, strain of conservatism, for they may also be read, despite their independent heroines, as cautionary tales about the underside of the feminist movement. As such, they reveal the tensions that prevail in American society about the issue of women's roles. In fact, to some degree they affirm traditional attitudes about gender.

Despite their resilience, resourcefulness, and independence, Clark's heroines find themselves in danger. Indeed, it may be their independence that makes them most at risk. Lacey Farrell, for instance, the only witness to a murder in *Pretend You Don't See Her* (1997), contributes to her dangerous situation by photocopying a key piece of evidence before she surrenders it to the police, and so, too, does *Moonlight Becomes You*'s Maggie Holloway (1996) by concealing a puzzling clue from authorities. Similarly, *You Belong to Me*'s Susan Chandler refuses to share information about the death of Regina Clausen with Donald Richards, a man with the professional expertise to assist her inquiry. In conducting their private investigations of crime, Clark's women, all of whom are utterly modern in their self-reliance and self-sufficiency, violate the rule of law and challenge the prerogatives of the essentially male criminal justice system. For doing so, they must to some extent pay through suffering. The implication of this plot line is clear: Women should rely upon traditional systems and organizations to protect the social order. In fact, their meddling is itself a disturbance of the social order, for it challenges traditional gender roles.

Perhaps nowhere does Clark make more clear the price of the disruption of traditional gender roles than in *You Belong to Me*. In this novel, independent women travelling alone on cruise ships become the targets of a serial killer. Grieving his own wife's death, Donald Richards has written a book about women who disappear. During a commercial break in the interview Susan Chandler is conducting with him, Richards observes that women are "particularly vulnerable" when they leave the secure worlds of "job and family" to strike out on their own into unfamiliar territory (23). Although the man who preys on such a woman is at fault, Richards claims, his statement implies the victim's culpability. Had she not been travelling alone, had she not stepped beyond the protective embrace of the familiar, had she not, in other words, violated traditional gender roles by claiming as her own the freedom of movement generally accorded to men, she might not have placed herself in the position to be victimized.

The novel's ending also to some extent reinforces traditional gender expectations in Clark's fiction. Although Susan Chandler actively participates in her own escape from death, it is her potential love-interest who assists in the rescue. In fact, Susan probably would have died had Donald Richards not persisted, despite her frequent rebuffs of his offers of assistance, in his efforts to save her. Law enforcement authorities, moreover, those representatives of male protection, are also involved in the rescue and apprehension of the criminal. On her own, a woman is incapable of restoring order.

Beyond this reassertion of male power and prerogative, however, is the novel's resolution in the conventional marriage plot, in the promise of the "they lived happily ever after" ending. Within the traditional family structure, women have been accorded the domestic role. In that role, they are expected to marry and to raise the children of their marriage, to create a comfortable home that may serve as a family haven, and to exemplify the civilizing virtues. Women have learned this role through observation and by custom; it is part of the process of social development that young girls experience. They learn it as well through the stories they read and hear, the fairy tales and romances that end with the hero's rescue of his beloved and their marriage. That plot shapes the expectations of many young girls, who will eventually assume their proper roles as wives and mothers.

Because she ends *You Belong to Me*, as well as the majority of her other novels, with the promise of marriage, Mary Higgins Clark clearly reinforces these traditional gender expectations. Susan Chandler may be a woman of achievement who has fashioned for herself a successful and satisfying career. She may have a circle of supportive and loving friends and family. But until she commits herself to a worthy male counterpart, her life is incomplete. Susan's regret about the life she never had with Jack certainly suggests that she feels marriage as the absence in her life. It is the missing element to complete fulfillment. The novel's final paragraph, moreover, in which Richards's embrace of Susan seems "the natural thing for him to do" (317), suggests that she has finally found that fulfillment in closure. At the dawn of a new millennium, and one preceded by three decades of a strong and an active feminist movement, Clark's novel thus testifies to the continued strength of these pervasive attitudes. If murder brings mayhem, so, too, *You Belong to Me* suggests, does a redefinition of gender roles, for it challenges the foundation of society's most fundamental social organization, the family.

In the end, Clark's novel of suspense, in keeping with the tradition of the genre, reasserts the principles of law and order in a world made chaotic by crime. Yet its message goes beyond the traditional by testifying to the value of domestic order as well. On the surface, Clark may seem to celebrate a thoroughly modern woman protagonist like Susan Chandler, but the subtext, or underlying literary markers, of *You Belong to Me* suggests a more traditional view of women's proper sphere. This work of popular fiction thus reveals some of the prevailing attitudes in American culture as the nation begins a new millennium.

We'll Meet Again
(1999)

In her sixteenth best-selling tale of mystery and suspense, *We'll Meet Again*, Mary Higgins Clark diverges a bit from her typical formula. Granted, contemporary social issues—in this case, health maintenance organizations (HMOs)—still give focus to certain plot elements and thematic concerns, and the intricately plotted tale hinges as usual on the life-or-death struggle of an endangered heroine.

Heroine, however, becomes heroines in *We'll Meet Again*, as Clark offers not one, but rather two central characters, both of whom must face the past to survive the present. The dual focus is an interesting but not entirely successful departure because neither character is fully realized. Molly Carpenter Lasch, the wrongly convicted heroine, would in any other Clark novel possess both the resourcefulness and the determination to save herself from harm. In this novel, however, she never quite triumphs over her victimization. Fran Simmons, the investigative reporter and old school friend who typically would play little more than a supporting role in Molly's drama, virtually upstages the intended protagonist—but without the proper resolution to her own search for self. In effect, *We'll Meet Again* promises more than it delivers, for plot rather than character drives this novel. Clark never entirely resolves the issues of personal growth and character development so clearly evident in the novel, and thus its conclusion is unconvincing and even unsatisfying. Molly and Fran may have escaped physical harm, but their psychological struggles have been explained away rather than acknowledged and overcome.

PLOT

We'll Meet Again begins with a brief prologue, a flashback to a sensational trial that occurred nearly six years before the novel's contemporary events. The flashback serves as a convenient plot device for conveying a great deal of necessary information in a compressed manner. The defendant, Molly Carpenter Lasch, is accused of murdering her husband, Dr. Gary Lasch, a prominent Greenwich, Connecticut, physician and founder of the Remington Health Management HMO, by crushing his skull with a heavy bronze sculpture. Her discovery that a young nurse, Annamarie Scalli, was pregnant with his child is the probable motive. Traumatized by the horror of the crime and the nature of her losses, Molly slips into dissociative amnesia and depression and, unable to recall the events of the evening on which she had returned unexpectedly early from seclusion at their Cape Cod retreat, can do little to defend herself. In the face of mounting evidence against her—she had, after all, been found in bed covered with her husband's blood—Molly agrees to plead guilty to manslaughter to avoid a murder conviction and is sentenced to serve ten years for her crime.

Five and a half years later, on the date of her release on parole from Niantic Prison, Molly's story begins again and moves relentlessly to its conclusion. Still unable to recall the events of her husband's death, Molly is nevertheless convinced that she is innocent of his murder and vows at a press conference to clear her name by discovering the truth. Among the reporters covering Molly's startling assertion is Fran Simmons, an anchor for the *True Crime* television series that now plans a feature on the Lasch case. Eager to scoop the competition, Fran hopes that old school ties will help her to gain Molly's confidence. She is surprised, nevertheless, when Molly telephones her to schedule an interview and equally astonished to discover that Molly, too, intends to make use of old school ties by enlisting Fran's investigative talents in her cause. Thus is born an alliance that will lead both to the brink of death.

The remainder of the plot focuses primarily on Fran's investigation of the six-year-old murder. The skeptical reporter is gradually convinced that Molly is indeed innocent of the crime. Unlike the police, who assumed from circumstances that Molly must have committed the murder, Fran explores inconsistencies—conflicting stories about an extra house key, for instance—and coincidences such as the murder of another doctor just two weeks before Lasch's death. She also digs into the status of Remington Health Management and its chief directors, the entrepreneur Calvin Whitehall and the physician Peter Black, to reveal other possible suspects and motives. She even uncovers some unsavory truths about Lasch himself. When Annamarie Scalli is found murdered in a restaurant parking lot following a meeting with Molly, only Fran believes in her friend's innocence of the crime. Fran knows that all is not as it seems at Lasch Hospital and that many people stand to lose a great deal if Molly is exonerated of Annamarie's murder. Exonerated, however, she will be, for in the world of Mary Higgins Clark, right prevails and criminals are punished. Fran's investigation leads to this inevitable but satisfying conclusion of every tale of mystery and suspense. The thrill of the genre is the getting there, and *We'll Meet Again*'s plot provides more than enough twists and turns to keep readers guessing.

Yet the very twists and turns of plot that constitute one of the novel's strengths account paradoxically for its weaknesses as well. Several of the subplots are underdeveloped or unresolved and thus seem unnecessary to the novel's central concerns. The subplot involving Dr. Adrian Lowe and the unethical medical experimentation conducted at Lasch Hospital, for instance, is certainly connected to the novel's thematic exploration of the corrupting nature of power, but the connection is neither convincingly nor fully developed. Similarly, the subplot about Fran's efforts to learn the truth about her father's embezzlement of a library fund and his subsequent suicide, which should be crucial to her character development, never quite leads to the self-knowledge that her quest seems to promise.

Equally unsatisfying is Clark's disclosure of the real murderer of Dr. Gary Lasch. One of the conventions of the mystery genre is that the reader must have equal opportunity with the detective to solve the crime. All the clues, in other words, must be present. In *We'll Meet Again*, however, Clark does not play fair with her readers. She never really provides sufficient evidence to link criminal to crime, so the revelation of the murderer's identity is not only surprising but also disappointing. The least likely of suspects, the murderer seems to be the culprit simply to fulfill plot needs. Someone other than Molly, after all, must have committed the crime, and the person least likely is as good as, if not better than, anyone else is. Certainly it guarantees a surprise, but it also leaves the reader feeling cheated of the opportunity to match wits with the investigator.

CHARACTER DEVELOPMENT

If *We'll Meet Again*'s plot is not entirely without flaws, then neither, rather surprisingly for a Mary Higgins Clark novel, is its characterization. Clark's typical heroine is an intelligent, independent, and forthright woman in her early thirties, frequently a successful young professional loved and admired by friends and colleagues for her genuine sincerity and quiet competence. Pulled by circumstances into danger and intrigue, she generally draws upon her own wits and force of character to face the unknown terrors that threaten her life, seldom requiring the assistance of others, especially a man, to rescue her from menace. In fact, danger usually strengthens her resolve and sometimes leads her to discovery of untapped personal resources.

As Clark initially presents them, the heroines of *We'll Meet Again* are typical of this pattern. Molly Carpenter Lasch may just have spent five and a half years in prison for a crime she did not commit, but when paroled she announces her intention to discover the truth and immediately sets about doing so. She secures an alliance with Fran Simmons, locates the missing Annamarie Scalli, and resists the advice and caution of friends and family who encourage her to forget the past and move forward in life. Similarly, Fran Simmons may harbor in her father's disgrace her own share of personal pain from the past, but she refuses to flinch from it. She keeps her family name when her mother remarries and seizes the opportunity to investigate the Lasch case not only because it is newsworthy but also because doing so will lead her back to the scene of that disgrace and the possibility of understanding it. United by personal tragedies that have blighted their lives, both Molly and Fran are determined to live on their own terms, whatever it takes to do so. For both, Clark's novel makes clear, the key to such a life lies in confronting the past.

The inevitable result of such a confrontation should be a deepening or expansion of self-knowledge, a sense of personal growth and development, and Clark clearly intends her heroines to experience such changes. In fact, she sets *We'll Meet Again* in the spring, with its promise of new beginnings, to underscore the point. However, as the novel's twists and turns of plot assume dominance, Clark seems to abandon this element of characterization. Fran's personal quest never quite reaches a climax, and Molly, faced with some disturbing revelations about her marriage and some distressing truths about herself, collapses into victimization. Clark may end the novel with the suggestion that both Molly, who has sold her

Connecticut home and accepted a publishing job in New York City, and Fran, who is clearly developing a relationship with a colleague who knows of her past, have overcome their personal struggles. That conclusion, however, seems unearned. Clark asserts it rather than dramatizes it, and thus it is ultimately unconvincing and even unsatisfying, a too-pat ending to real human trauma.

Molly's situation certainly illustrates the point. The privileged daughter of two loving parents, Molly, as Fran remembers her from their school days together at Cranden Academy, had always been a model of composure. "I remember thinking," she recalls, "if she met the pope and the queen of England at the same party, she'd know how to address them and in what order" (17). But her composure, Fran also believes, simply masks a shy and rather tentative young woman who seems "like a beautiful bird perched at the end of a branch, poised but ready at any second to take flight" (17). Molly confesses to Fran her admiration of her friend's strength and determination in the face of adversity (194), tacitly acknowledging those very weaknesses in herself and thus confirming Fran's evaluation of her. Molly may have seemed to possess the perfect life—a loving husband, a beautiful home, the ease and grace of moneyed security—but its foundation was uncertain because she herself was uncertain. Molly acknowledges this truth only after Annamarie Scalli tells her details of her affair with Molly's "perfect" husband.

Released from the prison of her past, Molly begins to assess herself. For the first time in her life, she questions her previous assumptions and faces some deeply submerged truths, most particularly her belief that frustration about her inability to bear a child was the source of the vague dissatisfaction she felt in her marriage (126). The implications of this self-assessment, troubling as they are to Molly, should lead to a reassertion of self that indicates character growth and development. If Molly were in fact a typical Clark heroine, they would indeed do so. In Molly's case, however, they merely undermine her sense of self, causing her to doubt her own identity (118) and to sink into depression. Rather than fight to save herself, she even contemplates suicide. Molly without illusions thus becomes the perfect victim. Unlike the typical Clark heroine, who draws strength from her discoveries, even her discoveries about self, and uses that strength to face adversity, Molly passively accepts what she comes to see as inevitable—revocation of her parole and conviction for Annamarie's murder. That passivity threatens her very existence. Given her character, it is not surprising that she survives her ordeal because others save her—almost from herself.

Undaunted determination and innate competence make Fran Simmons the more typical Clark heroine. In fact, when she faces her life-threatening situation, she not only saves herself but also the criminals—her essential humanity and sense of justice simply will not permit her to abandon them. Yet Fran's investigations have always been as much about self as about Molly. She, too, has harbored her own insecurities, never quite at ease as a teenager in the Molly Carpenter-world of Cranden Academy (18) and now, as an adult, angry at and embarrassed by her father's legacy. Investigating the Lasch murder will force her to return to the place so intimately connected to these insecurities, and Fran is, from the beginning, committed to her quest. "It's time," she thinks, to acknowledge the past; indeed, it may be "therapeutic" to do so (74).

Fran's journey of self-discovery, however, never quite reaches its destination, or at least it never seems to. Certainly, in the course of her investigations Fran learns that her father, whatever his crimes, had himself been the unwitting victim of fraud, knowledge that brings her some measure of comfort. She also forges a real friendship with Molly, whose charmed life she had so admired as an insecure teenager and whose affirmation of Fran's own admirable qualities both surprises and pleases the television journalist (194). Yet in the end, Fran seems virtually unchanged by her experiences and her newfound knowledge. She was and still is a competent professional committed to the good and true, and she is "still," as she confesses to herself, "licking [her] wounds" (367). The Lasch case had made victims of so many that vindication and triumph are virtually impossible for Fran, who cannot escape the shadow of sadness as she moves on in her life.

Clark's cast of secondary characters has one trait in common—power. Calvin and Jenna Whitehall, Dr. Peter Black, Dr. Adrian Lowe, even Dr. Gary Lasch, it will be revealed, seek to dominate others. Cal Whitehall, for instance, is a ruthless entrepreneur who, as Jenna tells Molly, considers "anyone or anything that causes him to lose money . . . the enemy" (65). The legacy of his humble beginnings, which included "bullying" by his father, is resentment of others' dominance. What he enjoys about his money is the power it gives him to control the lives of others. Similarly, Cal's beautiful and accomplished wife, Jenna, a successful lawyer in her own right, also knows the appeal of power. In fact, Cal is quite aware that much of his attraction for Jenna is his ability to give her the privileged life that power makes possible (90–91). The doctors in *We'll Meet Again* wield the power of life and death, so they, too, know what it is to dominate others. United by this single trait, these secondary characters constitute the evil presence in Clark's novel. Indeed, Clark will ground her primary thematic concerns in this aspect of characterization.

THEMATIC ISSUES

Power—its ability to corrupt and to destroy—is clearly the central theme of *We'll Meet Again*. Those who wield it have the ability to control and dominate. That ability, Clark's novel suggests, while holding the potential for good, is too easily perverted by human weakness. Too often, as Fran's colleague Tim Mason reflects, it makes others "the victim[s] of someone else's selfishness" (68). Clark's exploration of her theme, primarily through the vehicle of her secondary characters, certainly proves the point.

Resentment and jealousy fester beneath the attractive surfaces of both Cal and Jenna Whitehall and account in large measure for their abuse of power. Acutely aware of the advantages of others no more deserving than they, Cal and Jenna feel justified in getting what they want by whatever means necessary. Cal, who was abused as a boy by his father, uses his exceptional intelligence to attain the fortune that relieves him of the humiliation of "toadying" (43) to men of lesser talent and gives him the power to shape his own destiny. That power also gives him the ability to manipulate others. Cal soon finds that he quite enjoys playing games of cat-and-mouse with bewildered and frequently unsuspecting opponents, "[toying] with his prey while knowing all the time that it was a game he would win" (943) because he plays by his own rules (64–65). (At times, he even enjoys "toying" (43) with his wife, too.) The transition from acquiring companies to orchestrating murder seems inevitable in a man whose formative humiliations have essentially created an elegant thug with the power and authority to engender fearful respect (90).

In Jenna, Cal chooses the perfect marriage partner. Equally ambitious, she enjoys possession of her own "private territory" (90) achieved through her successful law career but values as well the "prestige" (91) that comes of being Mrs. Calvin Whitehall. She may disapprove of her husband's tactics and even at times resent his manipulation of her life, but she inevitably acquiesces to his demands, unwilling to sacrifice the benefits of her position (87–91). She has, after all, married him for them—and, in the process, betrayed her best friend, Molly Carpenter. That betrayal, however, bothers Jenna not a whit, and from her point of view, it should not. Molly, after all, has every advantage and all that she wants, including a husband she loves. Jenna thus has no scruples about using sexual power to attain her desires—both a powerful husband and a handsome lover (365).

Motives of another sort lie behind the corruption of the doctors' power in *We'll Meet Again*. Greed certainly accounts at least in part for Dr. Peter Black's willingness to participate in the unauthorized and unethical medical experimentation taking place at Lasch Hospital, but it does not account for the actions of Dr. Gary Lasch and Dr. Adrian Lowe. Rather, an innate sense of superiority (as well as the desire for fame), exacerbated by the power of life and death that they wield over suffering humanity, leads Lowe and his disciple Lasch to treat others with callous disregard for their individual integrity and intrinsic worth. They think nothing of testing experimental drugs on patients who are deemed to have outlived their usefulness or have become a financial burden on the health care system. If by chance someone should make a mistake, as the case of Natasha Colbert makes clear, the unfortunate error simply provides occasion for additional experimentation (338–43). The doctors in *We'll Meet Again*, with the financial backing of Cal Whitehall and Remington Health Management, thus confirm stereotypes of the omnipotent physician. They are convinced that their knowledge and power are not a trust but rather a license to exert control over others.

Power not only corrupts, Clark's novel makes clear, but also destroys, and its chief victims are the innocent and undeserving. Molly Carpenter Lasch will certainly bear the scars of her betrayal for the remainder of her life, but she at least survives. Other countless victims, including Annamarie Scalli, Jack Morrow, the principled doctor who intended to expose the corruption at Lasch Hospital, Natasha Colbert and her mother Barbara, and even to some extent Fran Simmons' father, do not share her good fortune. To the powerful, they are bothersome obstructions to their selfish desires or utterly expendable commodities, but Clark certainly does not share this view. The novel's conclusion exposes every cruelty and sees the antagonists punished for their crimes. It makes clear, in other words, that every person is worthy of a life, even the chronically ill or the psychologically troubled, such as Wally Barry, and that the corrupting nature of power is ultimately self-destructive.

Clark extends her primary theme through her critique of HMOs. Too many of these corporate enterprises, the novel makes clear, are like their powerful directors—concerned only about the profit margin, about what, in other words, they stand to gain from the enterprise. They shave services, cut personnel, and deny procedures and medications to some patients; some even dictate the length of time a doctor allots to a patient—

all in the name of cutting costs, which effectively translates into increasing profits. To deny care and treatment to the sick and infirm, however, is quite simply an abuse of power. It is "callous and alarming," warns Dr. Roy Kirkwood, a principled and dedicated physician who is choosing an early retirement because he is unwilling to comply with HMO demands that to him compromise patient care (217–20). The only solution to the problem, he maintains, is nonprofit HMOs run by doctors themselves (although certainly not doctors like Gary Lasch or Peter Black). Eliminating the profit incentive will help to prevent the unscrupulous from abusing the trust of their patients and ensure the health and safety of all.

We'll Meet Again clearly exemplifies the truth of the adage that power corrupts and absolute power corrupts absolutely. Human beings are simply too flawed to avoid exploiting an advantage, especially when every sort of human selfishness offers self-justification for their actions. In consequence, their institutions, their HMOs, for instance, are also subject to corruption, for they are simply reflections of the people who control them. Given these truths, the real wonder about humanity may be that people such as Fran Simmons and Molly Carpenter Lasch, people who possess genuine concern and compassion for others and who value truth and justice, exist at all. *We'll Meet Again* makes clear that they do.

A FEMINIST READING OF *WE'LL MEET AGAIN*

At the center of *We'll Meet Again* are three complex women, all of whom share the common experience of an education at Cranden Academy. The permutations of their friendships and the course of their adult lives thus figure prominently in Clark's novel. These subjects certainly offer fertile ground to the feminist critic, who examines literature through the lens of gender and whose theoretical assumptions are fully defined in chapter 6. For the feminist critic, *We'll Meet Again* reveals much about the nature of gender roles and gender expectations in contemporary society.

As products of Cranden Academy, an institution that represents the values of a privileged and secure social world and that has put the "finish" on their personalities, Molly, Jenna, and Fran embody the ease, grace, and competence that signify success. Bright, articulate, and attractive, Jenna and Fran have achieved rewarding professional positions, and Molly has gained recognition for her unfailing support of both philanthropic causes and her husband's success. From all outward appearances, they seem content and happy with their lives. Yet beneath the pleasing surfaces of their existence lie some disturbing undercurrents of resentment, jealousy, un-

certainty, and despair that suggest that their education may not have prepared them for life as contemporary women. Certainly this is the case for
Molly Carpenter Lasch.

The "beautifully mannered little girl" (176) that Dr. Daniels, Molly's
psychiatrist, had watched at the country club is, as he now observes, "the
perfect product of breeding and quiet wealth" (177) who always does the
expected. After a brief but satisfying publishing career, she married well
and then, following a miscarried pregnancy, devoted herself to her husband's career, becoming the "perfect Martha Stewart-type hostess" (156),
and to attempting to bear a child (50). By her own reckoning, Molly is a
"good girl" (194). She even evaluates her performance in terms of the
schoolhouse, assigning herself an A-plus for predictability, one of the
qualities that her husband had particularly valued in his wife (195). This
is the life for which her education in conformity had prepared her, and
she had learned her lessons well.

When Annamarie Scalli tells her that Gary had sneered at his "boring
Stepford wife" (146), Molly begins to evaluate the reality of her "perfect"
marriage and finds that she had essentially subordinated her life to her
husband's and thereby sacrificed herself. Like the women in Ira Levin's
chilling 1972 novel of contemporary suburban life, *The Stepford Wives*,
Molly had become submissive and subservient, utterly conforming to the
demands of a male-dominated world and virtually unaware of the quiet
desperation that such an existence engendered in her. Only her desperate
longing for a child, who would have filled the emptiness of her social
whirl, gives evidence of the undercurrents of dissatisfaction with her life.
Only in retrospect, however, can Molly even begin to make such an admission (126).

Molly's education in conformity clearly prepares her to uphold the patriarchal system. Rather than complain of unhappiness, she channels her
energies into her husband's success; rather than confront her husband
about his infidelity, she retreats to Cape Cod until she can rein in her anger
and pain. Even after Annamarie tells her that Gary was not worth killing,
Molly assumes the blame for his failures, convinced that if she had been
another sort of wife he would not have grown tired of her. Clark's novel
suggests that "good girls" such as Molly will inevitably fall victim to male
dominance, to men who will use and abuse them by marrying them for
their money and connections, for instance, or by sexually seducing them,
as the example of Annamarie Scalli demonstrates. These women may also
fall victim to the predatory women who imitate them, as the example of
Jenna Whitehall suggests.

A "strong" woman who has already earned a partnership in a prestigious law firm, Jenna, as Molly confides in Dr. Daniels, "*loves* Cal's power," and like him, she lets "nothing [stand] in *her* way"(273). Manipulative and aggressive, Jenna is, in fact, the female version of her husband. Whatever she wants, she will have, including another woman's husband. Against such a woman, Molly, a self-defined "cream puff" (273), simply cannot compete. Indeed, she does not even suspect that they are in competition.

The irony of her position, however, especially through the lens of a feminist perspective, is that for all her aggressive self-assertion, Jenna tends to define herself by or be dependent on the men in her life. Her social status is clearly linked to her husband's wealth and power: As Mrs. Calvin Whitehall, she enjoys privileges and prestige that would be absent from her life as Jenna Graham. Aware of her situation, Cal exploits his wife's vulnerability, bending her to his will on several occasions in the novel; she inevitably submits to his domination (87–91; 171–73). She also submitted to the sexual domination of Dr. Gary Lasch because she needed him in her life. Marriage to Cal was a means to an end. Her affair with Gary was compensation. But when she learns that he has betrayed her, she realizes that their need was never mutual (365) and that she has been reduced to the status of jealous mistress. Jenna's relationships with men thus make clear that even the strongest women are no match for the predatory male.

We'll Meet Again also provides the feminist critic with a provocative glimpse of the complex relationships between women themselves. On one level, the bond between Molly and Jenna and the one that develops between Molly and Fran confirm certain stereotypes about female friendship, especially its importance in women's lives. These women trust in and rely upon each other not merely for physical support but also for emotional comfort. They confide in each other their dreams and hopes, their doubts and fears, and draw strength from the bond that such confidences forge between them. Following her release from prison, Molly, for instance, relies on Jenna's unconditional acceptance to help ease her transition back into her interrupted life, and she gradually takes similar support from Fran, the lone voice that echoes Molly's protestations of innocence. Fran, too, benefits from her friendship with Molly, whose confession of admiration affirms the television reporter's rather compromised sense of self.

On another level, the novel's female friendships also reveal the unspoken rivalries that lie just beneath the surface of even the longest and closest relationships. Molly, for instance, is shocked by Jenna's confession of jealousy just as Fran is amazed by Molly's confession of admiration. Since their days at Cranden Academy, these women have been in competition with each other; they have measured themselves against each other and judged themselves inferior in some way. Jenna, for instance, recognized her diminished social stature in Molly's unconscious presumption of it, Fran saw in Molly's grace and poise the self-confidence she lacked, and Molly wished for Fran's determination, her strength in the face of adversity. Friends, it seems, become ideal images of self, each desiring something that the other has. Nothing bad need come of these desires; in fact, they can inspire constructive change in the self. But they can also lead to disastrous consequences. Female friendship, in other words, has the power not only to sustain but also to wound the self. It is a far more complex relationship than appearances suggest.

For all its flaws of plot and characterization, *We'll Meet Again* clearly has much to reveal to readers about both power and gender. What Clark says about these topics may be neither original nor unique, but the fact that these themes are important to her work is evidence that she continues to give weight and seriousness to a popular literary genre. Mystery and suspense, she seems to say, need not be only an entertainment. They can provoke readers to thought as well. *We'll Meet Again* certainly does.

9

Before I Say Good-Bye
(2000)

Grief, guilt, and the solitary self are not the usual suspects in novels of suspense. In fact, the murder and mayhem characteristic of such novels typically focus on a villain, the embodiment of evil, rather than states of mind and being. While Mary Higgins Clark's seventeenth best-selling novel, *Before I Say Good-Bye*, certainly has such a villain, whose discovery is central to the plot, the efforts to unmask him are also, and perhaps most importantly, the vehicle for explorations of another sort. In her novel, in fact, states of mind and being loom as powerful presences in the lives of the central characters and give shape as well to plot and theme. In her tale of a young woman's investigation into the mysterious circumstances of her husband's death, Clark probes these dark mysteries of the human heart and psyche, making them the true suspects of her interrogations.

Before I Say Good-Bye is the story of Cornelia "Nell" MacDermott, a thirty-two-year-old political commentator for the *New York Journal*. Married to an architect, Adam Cauliff, Nell leads the privileged life about which others dream. Family heirlooms furnish her Park Avenue apartment; designer clothes fill her closets; and as the beloved granddaughter of a revered retired congressman, she moves in circles of power and influence. When Adam dies in an explosion of his new cabin cruiser, however, Nell's world crumbles beneath her.

Determined to learn the truth about the mysterious circumstances of her husband's death, Nell assists the police in their investigations and even, despite an innate skepticism, enlists the aid of a medium who claims to be Adam's channel for transmitting messages from the beyond. Before long, Nell is confronting not only her devastating loss but also some wracking doubts about her relationship with her husband, who, she learns, may not have been the person she knew and thought him to be. She is also struggling for her life against a sinister force determined to prevent her from exposing calculated deceit and bloody murder.

PLOT

The three-part plot structure of *Before I Say Good-Bye* is key to Clark's control of her material. The novel's prologue, for instance, which takes place seventeen years before the contemporary events, at first seems unrelated to the mystery plot. In the prologue, a fifteen-year-old Nell finds herself caught in a dangerous riptide in the Maui surf that threatens first to drag her down to her death and then pulls her far out to sea. Released eventually from its powerful force, she swims valiantly toward shore, where her grandfather sits oblivious to her peril, but exhaustion taking its toll, she begins to slip beneath the waves. Then the miraculous occurs: Nell hears the voices of her dead parents urging her to fight (4). Buoyed by their encouragement, she finds the strength to battle not only the elements but also her own self-defeating lethargy and rides a wave to safety.

Despite its departure in time and place from the novel's main events, the prologue establishes a key element of both plot and character—psychic phenomena and Nell's sensitivity to them. At the moment of their death, readers learn in this prologue, Nell's parents had visited their daughter to say good-bye (2). Five years later they are still a presence in her life, and Nell remains acutely attuned to their spiritual presence. When, seventeen years later, Nell consults a medium after her husband's death, readers are not surprised because she does nothing out of character. Nor are they surprised when her parents appear again to safeguard their daughter's life. The prologue has made plausible the paranormal, so anything seems possible in Clark's novel.

Liberated from some of the constraints of physical reality, Clark can focus the body of her novel on its central mystery, and thus *Before I Say Good-Bye*, like other novels of mystery and suspense, the conventions of which are outlined fully in chapter 2 of this book, is a plot-driven literary work. To maintain the mystery and sustain the suspense, her chief purpose, Clark, like other writers of the genre, must provide just enough clues and a sufficient number of red herrings, or false clues, to keep hidden the identity of the criminal until the novel's final pages.

To achieve this end, she writes short, episodic chapters, each of which contains or seems to contain some vital information, but shifts the focus in each one. In chapter 44, for instance, Lisa Ryan, whose husband Jimmy was also killed in the cabin cruiser explosion, confides to Nell that she has discovered fifty thousand dollars hidden in his basement workroom. Chapter 45 shifts to George Brennan and Jack Sclafani, the police detectives investigating the case, and their interrogation of Adam Cauliff's former employer. Nell consults the psychic Bonnie Wilson in chapter 46, and the physician Dan Minor continues the search for his missing mother in chapter 47. While each of these episodes advances the novel's plot, arranged as they are, they are rather like a jumble of jigsaw puzzle pieces that have yet to be fitted together. Some pieces, in fact, seem to be missing. Others, readers eventually discover, are the novel's red herrings and belong in a different puzzle entirely. Both Peter Lang and Jed Kaplan, each of whom has reason to dislike Adam Cauliff, are high on the list of suspects in the crime. Neither, however, is guilty, so the chapters in which they feature, while they do provide some elements of characterization, actually obscure the identity of the real criminal. These shifts in focus clearly allow Clark to control the revelation of the various plot elements and thus to achieve her primary objective.

The novel's epilogue, which is set on Tuesday, November 7, a national election day, is unnecessary to the mystery plot. Nell had faced the villain and disclosed the truth months before. This short chapter, however, resolves the novel's secondary stories, or subplots. Nell achieves her dream, winning her grandfather's former Congressional seat. She also seems to have found true love. Before she says good-bye, Clark, in other words, provides her readers with the satisfaction of closure. Clark's is not an ambiguous world. Good, in fact, triumphs over evil in it and earns the rewards of right action. The novel's epilogue thus conveys a thematic statement in its resolution of plot.

CHARACTER DEVELOPMENT

As the embodiment of good, Nell MacDermott is *Before I Say Good-Bye*'s protagonist, or central character. She may aspire to political office and have experience of the political game, but dirty politics will never taint her image. Forthright and honest, she wants only the privilege of serving others and needs neither the power nor the glory that comes of political position because she already possesses them. She is, after all, the beloved only grandchild of Cornelius "Mac" MacDermott, who had served his Manhattan congressional district for fifty years before his retirement, and she airs her political views in a weekly newspaper column, "All Around the Town." Access to a trust fund established by her parents, anthropologists who were killed in a plane crash in the Brazilian jungle when she was ten years old, has given Nell a comfortable independence, but it has not compromised her innate generosity of spirit or her sensitivity to the needs of others. Nell is, in other words, Clark's typical heroine—intelligent, spirited, resourceful, and compassionate. She is a woman who deserves readers' sympathies.

Nell's golden life, however, has not been without its dark clouds. Despite her grandfather's loving care and the equally tender support of his sister, her Aunt Gert, following her parents' deaths, Nell feels her solitary self. The only child of only children, she has missed the warm embrace of an extended family and the sense of connection that it provides, and she has never had anyone in whom to confide her feelings. Nell's poise and self-assurance thus conceal a sense of loneliness and vulnerability that she seldom acknowledges even to herself.

Two powerful men dominate Nell's life, and Nell, who wants to please both, frequently feels that she "[walks] a tightrope" (32) between them. The first is her grandfather, Cornelius "Mac" MacDermott. At eighty-two, the retired congressman remains active in party politics, and nothing would bring him greater satisfaction than to see his granddaughter fill his former seat. In fact, he has "groomed" Nell to assume his congressional seat since she was a teenager (12). Forthright and honest, Mac has little tolerance for deceit, so he never quite trusts Nell's husband, Adam Cauliff, whom he regards as a "prime example of the difference between appearance and reality" (21). Utterly pragmatic, Mac has even less tolerance for ambiguities. He believes, in fact, in physical realities, not the "channel-babble nonsense" (58), as he puts it, to which his seventy-five-year-old sister Gert gives credence. Such a man, no matter his love for her, demands much of Nell, and as much as she loves him, she must keep secret from him some things about her life, particularly her own paranormal experiences.

Nell's marriage to architect Adam Cauliff, the other man in her life, leads to her precarious balancing act. From the beginning, Mac mistrusts the secretive stranger who seems less than he appears, and as Nell eventually discovers, his instincts are right on target. Nothing except his "inflated ego" and "unrealistic opinion of his own potential" (126) proves true about him and his life. "Hard as nails" (75), Adam is calculating and manipulative and therefore dangerous. He will do anything, even stage his own murder, to achieve his ends. To Nell, however, as well as his secretary, Winifred Johnson, the medium, Bonnie Wilson, and even Aunt Gert, he is utterly charming, the "master of the small courtesies" (296), which, of course, cost nothing. Within three months of meeting him, Nell marries this man who "[makes] her feel special" (261). His death devastates her.

Clark unfolds the story of Nell's and Adam's courtship and marriage slowly over the course of the novel in a way that suggests that the nature of their relationship is the true mystery of *Before I Say Good-Bye*. Thus their relationship functions as an element of both character and theme in the novel, and both are inextricably related to each other. Both are also related to the question that Nell eventually asks herself, "What had attracted her so totally to Adam?" (260). The answer, she realizes, was her need to be loved. During her long night of soul-searching about her relationship with Adam in chapter 63, Nell acknowledges for the first time that she may not have been in love with her husband. Instead, she may simply have wanted to be in love with him (263). While her friends were marrying and starting families, she had yet to find a partner, and then Adam entered her life. So ready was she for love, so desperate, in fact, was she for love, that she was vulnerable to his charms. His profession of love was sufficient to make her love him.

Nell's need for love is clearly a key element of her character, giving shape, however unconsciously, to her life. That need links her, much to her own surprise, to another of Adam's victims, Winifred Johnson. Disappointment has blighted the fifty-two-year-old secretary's life. She may once have won swimming trophies, but she has never been able to please her demanding mother, not even in adulthood. Nor has adolescent achievement translated into adult success. Quietly efficient, the unprepossessing woman seldom receives notice for her efforts, a situation that fuels her resentment of imagined slights, a tendency that she acquired from her parents. A woman such as Winifred, who is, like Nell, hungry for love, is equally vulnerable to the attentions of a charming man such as Adam, so her participation in his bid rigging and bribery schemes is understandable. She loves Adam and is willing to do anything he asks. After all, as Harry and Rhoda Reynolds, they already masquerade as husband and wife, and she fully expects that someday she will find happiness in marriage to him.

What motivates Adam to lie, cheat, steal, and kill is less obvious. Here, in fact, Clark's characterization is rather too pat. She gives readers a litany of his immoral and even criminal behavior when, in chapter 82, detectives receive a background report on his life, but a "broken home" (34) is an easy explanation for Adam's behavior. So, too, is the label "sociopath" (242). Certainly Adam lacks any regard for others. He is, after all, a man who must be chided by his wife to donate his old clothes to charity (246). But an unhappy childhood does not transform most people into criminals, as the example of Dan Minor makes clear.

A man whose burn-disfigured arms give evidence of a tragic childhood accident that prompted his mother to abandon him to his grandparents' care, Dan Minor has not permitted bitterness and resentment to shape his life. Instead, he has responded to his personal tragedy by becoming a pediatric surgeon who specializes in the treatment of burns. He has also never stopped searching for the mother who loved him too much to hurt him again. In fact, his search for his mother has been a primary factor in his decision to relocate from Washington, D.C., to New York City. He needs her to know that he never stopped loving her and never blamed her for his pain and hopes to bring peace to her life.

Dan does, of course, enter Nell's life, and his differences from Adam, despite his own childhood tragedy, could not be more pronounced. Selfless where the other man is selfish, compassionate where the other man is cruel, Dan wants nothing from Nell but her love. In fact, this physician will help to heal the heartsickness that Adam had caused her. Dan thus stands in stark contrast to Adam and thereby exposes a weakness in Clark's characterization of her villain.

Clark's interest, however, is clearly Nell, not Adam. In fact, he only physically appears in the novel's opening and concluding scenes. For nearly the whole of the novel, readers know him primarily through Nell's reminiscences and secondarily through others' testimony. This use of point of view, or the perspective from which readers see the novel's events, makes Nell the protagonist of *Before I Say Good-Bye*. She will grow and change and achieve self-knowledge during the course of her ordeal. All the novel's other characters are secondary to her.

THEMATIC ISSUES

The thematic issues of *Before I Say Good-Bye* evolve almost entirely from Nell's primary position in the novel. Chief among them is the aspect so crucial to her characterization—the need for love. In fact, to emphasize her point, Clark attaches the same aspect to Winifred Johnson and Dan

Minor, both of whom, like Nell, are "heart-hungry" (294). Granted, loving grandparents may have nurtured Nell and Dan to adulthood, but they still feel an essential isolation. They experience their solitary status not as solitude, as an inner peace derived from self-sufficiency, but as sad loneliness and disconnection from others. Nell, for instance, may have had a busy and exciting life, but at the end of the day, it is no substitute for the self-affirmation derived from the knowledge that another person has chosen to love her for herself, and not because she is a daughter or granddaughter. Similarly, professional satisfaction does not prevent Dan from seeking to regain the mother's love that had sheltered him as a small boy. Love is the emptiness in their lives, just as it is in Winifred's. That woman's need for another, in fact, is so great that it leads her into criminality. She will do whatever Adam asks to have his love.

"Heart hunger" is the dominant theme in Clark's novel, and as her term suggests, it is a need that lies at the core of human existence. Food and shelter may sustain the body, but love nurtures the soul. It affirms the self through connection to another whose own satisfaction depends upon the beloved's. It fulfills the self as nothing else can. The need for love can thus lead to vulnerability of the sort that the unscrupulous Adam exploited in his victims from Nell to Winifred and perhaps even to the medium, Bonnie Wilson. Yet it can also resolve itself into the altruism of a Dan Minor or the entire MacDermott clan, all of whom seek love to give it. Love, Clark makes clear in *Before I Say Good-Bye*, affirms human life and gives meaning to human existence. It is the very essence of being.

One of the novel's secondary themes—the nature of grief—also emphasizes Clark's main point, for as she dramatizes it, the death of a loved one is a sort of death of the self. Cut loose from the moorings of love, those who survive drift aimlessly in the daily minutiae of life, responding automatically to its demands to avoid being engulfed in the pain of loss. Adam's sudden and unexpected death is at first an unreality to Nell. His smell still permeates his clothing; his things still profess his being. Her memories still give him life, so Nell cannot weep, cannot grieve. She shores herself up by focusing on the inconsequential. On the night of Adam's death, she moves about their apartment arranging magazines and straightening pillows, preoccupied about tables and chairs and carpets and her Aunt Gert's naïve trust in others (58–63). Because she needs Adam to be alive (60), she cannot accept his death, and when, after a dark night of the soul, the first of many, she finally cries, her tears are as much for herself as for Adam. "Once again," she knows, "she had to become used to living without someone she loved" (63). She has to experience again the death of the heart.

Lisa Ryan's experience of the death of her husband, Jimmy, in the same boat explosion that kills Adam mirrors Nell's own. A paralyzing disbelief and the need to care for her three children keep Lisa focused initially on the routine business of life, and the model of their dream house, lovingly crafted by Jimmy's own hands, still testifies to the bright future they had planned. As disbelief gives way to despair and worry, Lisa begins to lose weight, a physical representation of the loss of self that results from the death of a loved one. Lisa's love of her children, however, who are themselves bearing grief's burden and thus need her to be strong, keeps her from utter collapse. So, too, does her need to resolve her uncertainties about Jimmy's character, and by extension the nature of their love, yet another way in which her response to grief mirrors Nell's. Both, in other words, find it difficult, as the novel's title suggests, to "say good-bye" to their loved ones.

Indeed, the novel's title, *Before I Say Goody-Bye*, implies the complex nature of grief and speaks to Clark's understanding of the emotion. On the one hand, those who survive a loved one need closure. They need to "say good-bye," according to Aunt Gert, who had comforted Nell following her parents' deaths (85), in order to free both the living and the dead. On the other hand, saying good-bye gives pain and thus proves difficult, so the living, who need the beloved, prolong their farewells. Before they say good-bye they must right a reputation, reveal a truth, mend a quarrel, or speak their hearts. They must, in other words, redeem the past. "The dead," as Nell admits to herself, "have a real presence in our lives" (137), one that gives comfort to grief, and for that reason, the saying good-bye, the letting go, is ever complicated. In fact, the whole paranormal dimension of Clark's novel, which was perhaps no more than an unusual plot device, actually functions thematically as well, suggesting that for some the saying good-bye is virtually impossible.

A second minor theme of *Before I Say Good-Bye* explores another human emotion—guilt and its accompanying need for redemption. Nell's quarrel with Adam the morning of his death, for instance, complicates her grief at his loss. Had she been able to apologize to him, she might have been able to say good-bye (58; 63), but death had preserved forever the fight between them, denying her the balm of forgiveness. Guilt is also the source of Dan Minor's separation from his mother. When a drunken stupor prevents her from rescuing her six-year-old son from the fire that disfigures him for life, Kathryn Quinn Minor flees to the anonymity of

New York City, where she battles depression and alcoholism and becomes the homeless woman known on the streets as "Quinny." Years later, a social worker reported that Quinny had once confessed that what she most wanted in the world was redemption (140). Her son, Dan, has devoted much of his adult life to finding her so that he might offer the love she had never lost, the forgiveness she never needed. Yet Quinny had clearly felt a burden of guilt so overwhelming that it had blighted the lives of both her and her son.

Each of these examples illustrates the novel's point about the burden of guilt, but Clark develops it most clearly through the example of Jimmy Ryan, a man so wracked by guilt that his death in the boat explosion is essentially a suicide. Until he loses his job because his employer overhears him commenting on the use of substandard building materials and speculating about graft in the company, Ryan works in the construction industry and enjoys an honorable and happy life. After two years of unemployment, however, having been blackballed in the business, he finds himself burdened by debt and willing to compromise his principles to reclaim the bright future that had once seemed so possible. Setting fire to an empty building seems harmless enough, especially if it secures his job, but when he learns of the homeless woman who had died in the blaze, Ryan realizes that the fifty thousand dollars that his employer had paid him for the job could not erase his guilt or redeem his remorse. In fact, when the bereaved Lisa finds the bundles of blood money stacked neatly beneath some papers in Jimmy's file cabinet, she begins to understand the source of her husband's depression in the weeks preceding his death. She also begins to think that Jimmy's whispered "I'm sorry" on the morning of his death (31) was a sad farewell. The man burdened by guilt may have known his fate when he stepped aboard Adam's cruiser, but he preferred death to his compromised life.

Clark imbues her fiction with a clear moral vision. She understands that even good people, such as Nell, cause hurt and do wrong, but because they are capable of regret, because, in other words, they acknowledge their errors and seek forgiveness, they are not criminals, but merely human. Criminals, however, do indeed exist. They are, for Clark, people with so little regard for others that they prey upon their goodness or pervert their weaknesses, and they range from the petty Jed Kaplan to the monstrous Adam Cauliff. Kaplan, for instance, is an ungrateful son who verbally abuses his mother for selling his future inheritance, a New York property, at a price that he believes is less than its value. Like Adam, of whom he is merely a lesser version, he believes himself entitled to his desires and despises those who earn their success. Adam, of course, is the successful version of Jed. His polished surface, however, merely conceals a savage selfishness. Adam uses Nell's love to secure his fortune and manipulates Winifred's need to conceal his plan. Cold and calculating, he murders anyone who poses an obstacle to his desires and even stages his own death to escape the consequences of his acts. Such persons, the utterly amoral, earn Clark's, and readers', contempt. Yet individuals are not alone in her condemnation.

Clark has frequently directed her criticism at abuses in the business world. *The Cradle Will Fall* (1980), for instance, explored the legal and ethical issues surrounding the fertility industry, and *While My Pretty One Sleeps* (1989) revealed some of the abuses of the fashion world. *Before I Say Good-Bye* offers an indictment of corruption in the construction industry. Bid rigging and bribery schemes are merely forms of murder in this novel. When builders cut costs by using substandard materials, façades are bound to collapse, injuring innocent passersby (195). When millions are within the grasp of the unscrupulous, someone will inevitably pay the price. The Peter Langs, the Sam Krauses, even the Walters and Arsdales of the construction industry are all prey to human greed, the blight of any business, and Clark makes it clear that such "civilized" (192) criminality deserves far more punishment than a few hours of community service or even a hefty fine—paid with the profits of graft.

Clark's sympathies lie, as always, with the good and honest and upright. Certainly they may slip, as Jimmy Ryan does, but when they do, they feel genuine remorse for their fall and try to rectify their mistakes. When Lisa Ryan asks Nell to dispose of the fifty thousand dollars that Jimmy himself could not bear to spend, she not only redeems his goodness but also epitomizes Clark's essential faith in humanity. Indeed, her moral vision resides in this faith. Her novels speak to it.

A PSYCHOLOGICAL READING OF *BEFORE I SAY GOOD-BYE*

As a novel that uses psychic phenomena as a plot device, *Before I Say Good-Bye* certainly lends itself to a psychological interpretation. Critics using this approach apply the methods of the psychoanalyst to the study of literature. They examine the minds of a novel's characters to explain motivation and actions and seek in psychology the secrets of the literary work. This perspective is particularly appropriate to a novel that explores states of mind and being through its use of the psychological motif of the double.

In his revolutionary study of the human mind, Austrian neurologist Sigmund Freud (1856–1939), founder of the field of psychoanalysis, essentially argued that the psyche is actually a composite of both conscious perceptions and unconscious urges and that unconscious needs and desires, or instincts, exert a powerful behavioral force on the "self," a force that is as strong as any conscious or physical need. Freud divided the psyche into three parts. The id, he explained, is that part of the unconscious that is primitive and dominated by primary urges. It seeks immediate gratification of every desire and impulse, even those that may be self-destructive. Its opposite is the super-ego, that part of the psyche that creates an ideal self and that also functions as a conscience, registering approval or disapproval of one's thoughts and actions. Mediating between the two is the ego, the "self" that the individual projects to the world and which each person believes to be his or her reality, the conscious "self."

From Freud's explanation of the psyche and his description of what is essentially a composite self come as well the notion of the double. Sometimes called the alter-ego or mirror image, the double objectifies a concept of the divided self that developed in the twentieth century and suggests the internal struggle between opposing selves within the individual. In literary terms, the double, which is sometimes known by its German equivalent, *Doppelgänger*, is a device whereby a character is self-duplicated. In other words, two different characters represent the same character. Two famous examples of the use of the double occur in Robert Louis Stevenson's *The Strange Case of Dr. Jekyll and Mr. Hyde* (1886) and Joseph Conrad's *Heart of Darkness* (1899/1902). Stevenson's Jekyll, the respected doctor, and his Hyde, the vicious criminal, are in reality one individual divided against himself. The characters have given rise to the phrase "Jekyll and Hyde personality." Conrad's narrator, Marlowe, discovers his double, Captain Kurtz, during a journey into uncharted territory that symbolically represents the unconscious, and thus the two characters are essentially one. As these examples suggest, use of the double allows writers to give depth to their explorations of their characters' psychology, and Clark, who had previously used the device in novels such as *Loves Music, Loves to Dance* (1991) and *I'll Be Seeing You* (1993), puts it to good effect in *Before I Say Good-Bye* to reveal Nell's unconscious motivations for marrying Adam.

If the true mystery of *Before I Say Good-Bye* is indeed Adam's appeal for Nell, then the explanation may lie in what Nell mistakenly perceives as a "shared sense of isolation" (111). Like Adam, Nell is an only child. But she is also an orphan. Her solitary state is thus not a matter of choice, and she experiences it as an emptiness, one that has essentially defined her sense of self. Despite the love of her devoted grandfather and great-aunt, she feels the pain of loneliness rather than the peace of solitude, and she longs for a love that will fill her empty spaces. To some extent, Nell is two selves: one confident and content, the self Nell projects to the world; the other sad and vulnerable, the self Nell hides from others. In fact, Nell seldom admits the existence of this other self, so adept is she at projecting her ideal image.

In Adam, Nell believes that she has found a soul mate, someone like her who will complete her life. Adam's isolation, however, is not a matter of circumstance but of choice. Where, Nell wonders at his memorial service, are his friends and colleagues, those who, like her, grieve his loss? The answer, quite simply, is that they do not exist. Adam had severed all human ties by lying, cheating, and stealing his way to success. He had even as a teenager been questioned about the death of a wealthy uncle (341). A man such as Adam draws strength from his isolation. It places him outside the bounds of society and thereby justifies his behavior. He need care only about himself because nobody cares about him. Winifred Johnson, Bonnie Wilson, and even Nell MacDermott matter only so long as they are useful to him. Adam's isolation, then, is not like Nell's, and what she embraces in her husband is not a soul mate but an outlaw image of self that emphasizes separation rather than relation. It is destructive and even self-destructive. Before Nell can say good-bye to it, however, she must acknowledge its existence. She must, in other words, confront her other self to achieve psychic wholeness.

Nell's investigation into Adam's life is thus a discovery of self. In fact, from the point at which she questions the nature of her relationship with her husband, and particularly in two key chapters, 63 and 70, she must acknowledge that it had been rather destructive of the self she knew as hers. Nell had, for instance, dreamed of assuming her grandfather's congressional seat (13–14; 259), but Adam's disapproval had dissuaded her from pursuing a political career. Had her "fears and misgivings," she wonders, "her confusion and doubt and self-questioning" been a response to Adam's "negativity" (259)? Her marriage, she admits to herself, had not fulfilled her as she had hoped, and she had not regretted the weekends that Adam spent on his cruiser because she had "enjoyed the time alone" (263). For Adam, she had invaded her trust fund (261), curtailed her visits with Mac, and shelved her career goals. She had sacrificed much for love (294), she realizes. What she had essentially sacrificed, however, was herself. Examining a portrait, "too large for her taste" (295), that Adam had had painted of their wedding picture, Nell remarks her "lifeless" smile and Adam's own "flat" expression and wonders whether the artist had indeed captured the truth about her life with Adam: In her marriage, Nell MacDermott had virtually ceased to exist (295).

As Nell sorts dispassionately through her memories, Clark's recurrent motif is invasion. Adam had invaded her space, her self, transforming it, and her, into unfamiliar territory. Nell's anxieties about space thus symbolize her deep psychological unease about her own identity. She begins to reclaim her sense of self on the morning that she empties Adam's dresser and then returns the bedroom furniture to its premarital position, unexpectedly achieving a "renewed familiarity" with the room that gives her a "sense of sanctuary" against her grief and pain (233). As she admits the truth about her relationship with Adam, however, Nell deliberately erases him from her life by rearranging each room of her apartment. First she reorganizes her books, which Adam had a habit of pulling from the shelves and replacing "willy-nilly," so that her favorites are again "within easy reach of her comfortable club chair" (259). A day later, having awakened "with the sensation of having come home" (275), Nell packs away the clothes in her husband's closet, discards the spider plant that she did not like, a birthday gift from Adam, and removes from its place above the mantle the wedding portrait that had never suited her taste. With these acts, "all traces of Adam had been expunged from the living and the dining rooms" (295). The "strange land" (275) that now stretches out before her is the territory of self, and no longer constrained by the limits imposed by Adam, she is free to explore the whole of her terrain.

By the end of *Before I Say Good-Bye*, as the novel's epilogue makes clear, Nell has indeed bid farewell to her other self, but not before she has examined it fully through her relationship with Adam. She has also bid farewell to the grief that has shadowed her life since her parents' deaths. It was that grief that had made her sad and lonely and left her to feel isolated from others. It was that grief that had led her to embrace isolation in Adam, the man she had mistakenly perceived as her double. But whereas Adam was ruthless and manipulative and wanted selfish control of others, Nell is generous and compassionate and wants only to love and be loved. She wants relation, in other words, not isolation, and she finds all that she wants in service to her constituency and within the circle of family and friends. Nell learns much about herself in *Before I Say Good-Bye*. Indeed, her election victory is a ringing endorsement of the person she is.

On the Street Where You Live
(2001)

"The good old days" is for many the wistful refrain to the chaos of modern life. Amid days packed full of appointments and voicemail and e-mail messages, of sandwiches eaten on the run and crowded commutes to the office, people long for a time when the pace of life moved slowly, when they could nurture family and friendships over proper meals and communal gatherings. Amid the daily litany of murder and rape, of drive-by shootings and incidents of road rage broadcast on the evening news, they long as well for a time when it was unnecessary to lock every door and window of the house to protect both their possessions and themselves from harm, when electronic security systems and surveillance cameras had yet to be invented because nobody could imagine needing them. Yes, the safety and serenity of "the good old days" offer an attractive alternative to the disquieting and disorienting modern world—or do they? This is the question that Mary Higgins Clark explores in her eighteenth best-selling novel of mystery and suspense, *On the Street Where You Live*. Her answer is itself a bit disquieting.

Set amid the stately Victorian houses of Spring Lake, New Jersey, *On the Street Where You Live* explores the connections between the past and the present, a common Clark theme, through the life of its central character, Emily Graham. A criminal defense attorney, Emily moves to Spring Lake from Albany, New York, and takes up residence in the Shapley house, a lovingly restored Victorian where her great-great-grandmother had grown to adulthood. For Emily, who is leaving behind her a string of disappointments and even personal threats to assume a new position in New York City, Spring Lake and especially the Shapley house make her feel as if she has come home. The discovery of two bodies buried in her backyard, however, quickly dispels Emily's peace of mind. So, too, does the discovery of two more bodies and evidence that a stalker has targeted Spring Lake's new resident.

Within days of her arrival, Emily is straddling both the past and the present as she investigates a series of parallel murders. In each case, one murder occurred in the 1890s, the other more than a hundred years later. One of the victims, moreover, is Emily's great-great-grand aunt, Madeline Shapley, who had disappeared from Spring Lake one sunny day in 1891. A serial killer, it seems, had once preyed upon the town's unsuspecting young women. Now another seems to be copying the first, and it appears as if Emily may be his next victim. To save herself, she must discover the link between the murders, for the key to the present, she realizes, most certainly lies in the past.

PLOT

Clark organizes the plot of *On the Street Where You Live* around not one series of events but two—the mysterious disappearances of several young women more than one hundred years apart—and uses it both structurally and thematically. She had used this narrative strategy before, in her 1994 novel *Remember Me,* and to similar effect. In that novel, Menley Nichols, who has never stopped blaming herself for the death of her two-year-old son, Bobby, spends a month living in Remember House, an eighteenth-century landmark on Cape Cod, Massachusetts. There she discovers the house's sinister tale of betrayal and abandonment, a tale that begins to assume eerie reality as Menley starts to live the story of Remember House's previous occupant, Mehitabel, whose ghost is said to haunt the widow's walk, waiting for her infant daughter's return. Menley, like Emily in *On the Street Where You Live,* must thus solve the mysteries of the past to understand the present.

In *On the Street Where You Live,* those mysteries focus on the disappearances and presumed deaths of three friends, Madeline Shapley, Letitia Gregg, and Ellen Swain, in the 1890s. One hundred and ten years later, their case files remain open but forgotten until the day that construction workers unearth the body of Martha Lawrence in the Shapley house backyard. In her hand, she clutches Madeline Shapley's finger bone. The connections between these women gradually become more than coincidence. Both had disappeared on the same date, September 7. So, too, had Letitia Gregg and Carla Harper, who had gone missing on August 5 over one hundred years apart but whose bodies are now discovered buried together beneath the holly tree at 15 Ludlam Avenue. All indications are that another victim will join Ellen Swain in her unknown grave on the anniversary of her death on March 31, a date that looms forebodingly just ahead. As Emily sifts the evidence and researches the past, coincidence resolves into premeditation, at least on the part of the contemporary killer, and eventually past and present merge in the killer's form. Clark has thus written a tale of two mysteries, and their parallel plots have provided a structure for the novel's events. They have also raised thematic issues that will be explored later in this chapter.

The novel's cavalcade of suspects is yet another narrative element that effectively creates a second set of parallel plots, both involving Emily. One set of characters—Joel Lake, one of Emily's former clients, and Ned Koehler—factor in an ongoing story about a stalker who had been menacing Emily for more than a year in her former Albany, New York, home. After surveillance cameras that her friend Eric Bailey had installed in her home record Koehler's attempt to break in, police arrest and eventually imprison the unbalanced man in a psychiatric facility, and Emily begins to recover her sense of security. But shortly after her arrival in Spring Lake, she receives candid photos of herself that make clear that she is again the object of someone's obsession. Coming as it does in the immediate aftermath of the discovery of the first two bodies, she cannot be certain that the photo and the murders are unconnected, and neither can Clark's readers. And now she has far more suspects and far more danger to worry her.

Dr. Clayton Wilcox, for instance, makes Emily feel uncomfortable when she seeks his assistance with her research on Spring Lake's Victorian past (78; 222–25), but she would be even more unsettled if she knew that the former college president had once had an affair with an attractive young student. Robert Frieze, another suspect, whose string of infidelities attests to his attraction to beautiful young women, is experiencing troubling losses of memory that are even making him doubt his own innocence. And both men, as Emily significantly discovers, live in houses associated with the Victorian murders. When his frequent visits to Spring Lake eventually make Eric Bailey a suspect, Clark's second set of parallel plots merge into one, doubling the menace to Emily as well as readers' suspense.

Clark's parallel plots also help to create the suspense of *On the Street Where You Live* because one of their key elements is time. Both series of murders occur on the same dates, and the exact number of months and days that separated the original 1890s murders separates the contemporary murders. The novel's seemingly insignificant opening date, March 20, thus attains more importance after police have deduced the connections between past and present. A third murder seems inevitable to complete the symmetry of the plot, and by the time they realize the connection, they have very few days to catch a killer. Time becomes an enemy, not only the rapidly decreasing number of days until the next projected murder, but also the previous century that has buried clues and obscured motives. The race against time is one of Clark's common strategies to create and maintain suspense, and in *On the Street Where You Live*, Clark structures her plot, as she does in many of her novels, around the calendar, heading each section with a date and day of the week from Tuesday, March 20, to Sunday, April 1. Each calendar day is thus the signpost of danger ahead.

Another unsettling time element in Clark's novel is the irony implicit in its seasonal setting. Emily moves to Spring Lake on the day before the vernal equinox, or the first day of spring, the season associated with renewal and rebirth, so it seems a most auspicious time for her own new beginning. Blustery winds, however, and dreary gray skies rather than gentle warmth and blazes of color undercut the symbolic connotations of the season. So, too, does the discovery that murder and mayhem are among the town's inhabitants. While the world may seem to be "in balance" (18) as the novel begins—a comforting thought to Emily, the timing, in spite of what the calendar proclaims, is not quite right.

POINT OF VIEW

Clark's manipulation of point of view, or the perspective from which readers observe events, also contributes to the suspense of her novel. Clark generally chooses a third-person omniscient point of view. Her narrator, in other words, who is not a participant in the action, possesses the ability to relate events from the past as well as the present and has knowledge about all of the characters, including their thoughts. Such a point of view dominates *On the Street Where You Live*, each chapter shifting focus from character to character and revealing just a bit more information and thereby creating the jigsaw puzzle effect that keeps readers attempting to work out the proper fit between the various parts until the whole picture emerges at the novel's end.

Interspersed throughout the novel, however, are brief chapters in which the killer speaks in his own voice. These first-person narratives, as they did in previous novels where Clark used a similar technique, including *A Stranger Is Watching* (1978), *Stillwatch* (1984), *Weep No More, My Lady* (1987), and *You Belong to Me* (1998), reveal much about his personality and motivation. Readers hear him gloat, for instance, about police ineptitude and his victims' terror; they hear his anger and frustration when his plans go awry. Within the mind of the killer, they know as well his dark intentions. In other words, they have foreknowledge of the murders, something none of the novel's characters possesses, yet they are powerless to foil his plans. Instead, they must watch in horror as one character after another falls victim to this evil presence. From the foreknowledge and the anticipation that these first-person chapters create comes the novel's suspense.

CHARACTER DEVELOPMENT

Because people reveal much about themselves, both consciously and unconsciously, when they speak, the first-person narrative chapters in *On the Street Where You Live* provide special insight into the killer's character. A man who relishes "the thought of his omniscience" (16) and savors "his sense of supremacy over his victims" (15), the killer, readers learn early in the novel, genuinely believes that he is the reincarnation of the man who murdered Madeline Shapley and her friends a century before, Douglas Richard Carter. Armed with the journal in which Carter had recorded the details of his crimes, the contemporary villain, Will Stafford, is recreating the past. Indeed, he has become its recreation, for when Clark reveals his identity, he is dressed to resemble Carter, his great-grandfather, from his high-collared shirt and string tie to the thin mustache painted above his upper lip (303). At times, he even expresses himself in the formal language of the past. Anticipating the discovery of the second set of bodies, for instance, the killer thinks, "I am eagerly looking forward to the activity that I know will ensue later today" (157). Several days later, when he recalls his murder of Bernice Joyce, the elderly woman who he fears can connect him to the scarf he used to strangle Martha Lawrence, he confesses, "It has been a most distressing morning. . . . I had to make a radical and potentially fatal decision" (255). Such stilted sentence patterns and formal language make Will sound old-fashioned and create the illusion that he has indeed become his spiritual and psychological ancestor.

Will's double life extends beyond his identification with Carter. As Will Stafford, real estate attorney, he is also a man with two sides. With quiet competence and solicitous concern, he charms not only Emily Graham, but also Natalie Frieze, the discontented trophy wife of a local restaurateur, and even his secretary, Pat Glynn, all of whom he murders or intends to murder. Yet only Pat, who is too infatuated with her employer to acknowledge his iron will and stone heart when he orders his dying father from his office, glimpses the viciousness that lies beneath his fine manners and witty banter. Will, who toys with Pat's feelings and romances a married woman, adores the adoration of women, but he does not like them. Rather, he is a danger to them, and in that way, he is similar to another of the novel's characters, Eric Bailey.

Bailey, a "shy genius" (20) to those who know him, including Emily Graham, is actually an angry man who seeks revenge against those who have made him feel insignificant, especially women. Bailey may be a technological wizard who had launched a successful Internet company that had made him, and Emily, millionaires, but women have never found him attractive, seeing only a stammering and bespectacled socially inept man whose stooped shoulders reveal an innate lack of self-confidence. Expensive clothing is simply no substitute for personality, but Bailey lacks this understanding. He blames others instead for the hurt and humiliation that he experiences when they reject his advances.

When Bailey meets Emily, he becomes infatuated with her. She is, after all, the lawyer who had argued and won the struggling entrepreneur's case against a major software provider without asking for a fee. She had shared in his victory, too, for the seemingly worthless stock certificates that he had given her in payment were suddenly worth millions when he listed his company on the stock exchange. They had that in common, and certainly it was enough on which to build a relationship.

Emily, however, considers Bailey a younger brother, although he is in fact three days older than she (181), and while she appreciates his friendship and admires his intelligence, she is not romantically attracted to him. So when his Internet empire collapses, Bailey burns with resentment of Emily, who had sold her stock before the crash and thereby pocketed the profits of his efforts, blaming her, not himself, for his ruin. Before long, he is stalking her every move, first in Albany and then in Spring Lake, and as she becomes ever more unattainable, he becomes ever more determined to make her feel his humiliation.

The focus of Will Stafford's and Eric Bailey's twisted obsessions is Emily Graham, the protagonist, or central character, of *On the Street Where You Live*. Clark's typical heroine, she is a talented professional woman in her early thirties whose competence and intelligence are matched by her generosity and compassion and whose sudden wealth has not altered her essential self. In fact, little about Emily needs altering. A defense rather than a prosecuting attorney, Emily believes in people and in justice. She may not like the petty thief Joel Lake, for instance, but she will defend him because the evidence suggests that he did not commit the murder of which he stands accused. (And she has enough of a conscience to fret when he taunts her following his acquittal with the lie that he may have been guilty.) Such trust, however, does make her vulnerable to the selfish and the unscrupulous. In fact, she has lost both her husband and her best friend since college because they betrayed their bonds to her by engaging in an adulterous affair with each other. Now, in need of both a "change of direction and a change of pace" (18), Emily, wounded but resilient, has moved to Spring Lake to begin again. Before she can do so, however, she will have to learn some sad truths about life, truths that form the novel's thematic core.

THEMATIC ISSUES

The chief truth that Emily learns from her experience at Spring Lake and thus the central theme, or main point, of *On the Street Where You Live* is the continuity between the past and the present. Although the English novelist L. P. Hartley may have asserted in *The Go-Between* (1953) that "the past is a foreign country," according to Mary Higgins Clark, it merely seems so. The differences between two eras, she suggests, are primarily superficial, matters of style and taste and custom. Far more important for Clark are similarities of behavior and attitudes that link one generation to another and thereby define and indeed give substance to human civilizations. By focusing on these generational similarities, Clark challenges the romantic view of the past that leads people to restore its façades and revive its fashions in a futile effort to reclaim its perceived glories. In other words, by exploring people rather than artifacts, she effectively denies the very notion of the "good old days" for which so many long. Her backward glance is simply another view of her own time.

Spring Lake, for both its Victorian and contemporary residents, was and is an idyllic retreat from the world beyond its borders. Its Victorian houses, with their comforting substance and inviting front porches, look "secure and serene" (18) to Emily, just as they did to the generations who erected them. The "reassuring regularity" (38) of life in this prosperous resort, with its bracing sea breezes and dramatic vistas of the "silvery" Atlantic (14), seems the precious inheritance of that previous era. Cotillions and picnics and parlor games may have given way to cocktail parties and tennis dates, but both the 1890s and 1990s inhabitants of Spring Lake would have agreed that life in this "quietly beautiful" community "revived the soul" (13). The Gates family, for instance, as Emily learns when she reads Phyllis Gates's memoir, *Reflections of a Girlhood*, had once escaped Philadelphia's heat and humidity for the *"gentle life of summer residents"* (107) of Spring Lake. A century later, Emily Graham is not alone in her belief that life in this haven is worth the seventy-mile commute into New York City each day.

Phyllis Gates's memoir as well as the letters and diary of another Victorian Spring Lake resident, Julia Gordon, both of which Emily reads as she searches for clues to the current series of murders in evidence from the previous series, brings to life an "era of horse-drawn carriages" and "oil lamps" (88), of simple pleasures and innocent pursuits, all of which are now embodied in Spring Lake's Victorian houses. Many of Spring Lake's residents are living reminders of generational continuity who inhabit ancestral homes. The town's transplanted citizens, moreover, frequently devote both time and money to the faithful restoration of an old home. Clayton and Rachel Wilcox, for example, who moved from Ohio to Spring Lake when he retired as president of Enoch College, have furnished their period house, except for Dr. Wilcox's study, in the dark upholstery and heavy draperies characteristic of one style of Victorian-era décor, a style that Emily finds oppressive (78). Similarly, the previous owners of the Shapley house had devoted their three years there to lovingly recreating its Victorian splendors. In fact, they had even had restored twenty-seven pieces of the house's original wicker furniture, covering the cushions in fabric that they believed was a "replica of the original floral print" (108), and Emily is now eager to return them to their former home on her wraparound porch.

Spring Lake's Victorian houses clearly stand as symbolic representations of their era, and their restoration certainly gives evidence of its seductive appeal. To inhabit these houses is almost to be transported to that past, but that past, Clark makes clear, is largely an imagined past. It is the past as people want and need to remember it. It is a past that reassuringly distances them from current stresses and worries. Emily, for instance, purchases the Shapley house on little more than instinct. Although she had seen it for the first time only three months before taking possession of it, the house had long been a "vivid presence in her childhood imaginings— half real, half blended with fairy tales" (19). When, after several years of life "in the fast lane, and sometimes almost getting clobbered" (18), Emily first steps into the Shapley house, she knows "immediately that for her the place held a feeling of coming home" (19). Here, amid the remnants of a time that seems to her more magical and "so much more sheltered, so much less demanding" (221) than her own, Emily expects to find the "complete and total peace" (18) that she desires. Even after two bodies have been unearthed from her backyard and two others from another, Emily is "enchanted" (244) by the world that lives for her in Phyllis's memoir and Julia's letters and diary, and she has to remind herself that the world that she has imaginatively entered is not so different from her own. And indeed it is not.

As Emily conducts her investigations into the past, she uncovers a lurid tale of sexual predation and drug dependency concealed behind Spring Lake's Victorian façades, a tale not unlike the ones about which Reba Ashby reports in *The National Daily*. Madeline and Letitia and Ellen had all been murdered by a respected member of the community, a man who to all appearances provided devoted care to his invalid wife. That man, however, could not resist the beauty of a young woman, nor could he accept her rejection of his efforts to seduce her. What he could not possess, he killed. That wife, who was bedridden from crippling arthritis, was also little more than a drug addict. To relieve her pain, doctors had prescribed daily doses of laudanum, an opium derivative, that were far too strong for Mrs. Carter, and she lived her life in a "sedated state" (261), tears her only release. Such a woman may easily have been persuaded by her husband that Ellen Swain had indeed left their home alive on the day that she disappeared. Yes, the "good old days" of the Victorian era may seem earnest and upright. After all, young men and women observed strict courtship rules in those days. A young lady was "very proper and most circumspect in her behavior" (106) and would never think of revealing her feelings until she was certain of a young man's affection. But in truth, the era's proper manners and rigid mores, or behavioral standards, could also be empty gestures and meaningless forms, as superficial as Spring Lake's restored Victorian façades, for humans, no matter the era, are imperfect creatures.

As Clark's parallel plots make clear, no era is without its villains—or its senseless murders, its petty larcenies, its self-serving deceptions, its calculated cruelties. Will Stafford and Richard Carter are the most obvious examples of this truth, but Natalie Frieze and Richard Carter, both of whom appear to have married for money, are not so very different from each other either. And there must surely have been adulterous husbands like Clayton Wilcox and Bob Frieze, vindictive extortionists like Gina

Fielding, and shrewish wives like Rachel Wilcox in the past. Betrayal and hypocrisy, jealousy and revenge are not diseases of the modern era only. So while everyone may wish from time to time for the "good old days," *On the Street Where You Live* makes clear that those days exist only in the imagination. They are comforting fictions, as Emily's experience teaches her, but we have to live in the now.

Clark's references to reincarnation throughout the novel to some extent reinforce this final point. Will Stafford is convinced that he is the reincarnation of Spring Lake's Victorian serial killer (8). As such, he has reason to kill. He is reliving a previous existence; his actions are beyond his control. The notion of a reincarnated serial killer, however, certainly disturbs the psychologist Dr. Lillian Madden, for it contradicts a central tenet of the belief: "Reincarnation," as she tells her secretary, Joan Hodges, "is a form of spiritual growth." Thus, a serial killer in a previous life "would be paying for his transgressions now, not *repeating* them" if he were reincarnated (94). Will thus has no justification for his actions. He is instead responsible for his crimes, not only the murders he commits in Spring Lake, but also his attack on a young woman in Colorado during his adolescence, an attack for which he feels no remorse but rather blames his father for allowing him to spend three years in juvenile detention (177). Because Will has lived psychologically in the past since the day he discovered his great-grandfather's crime journal, he has avoided real engagement with the present, but in the end, he cannot avoid the judgment of the present. As Nick Todd, whose interest in Emily certainly offers romantic promise, tells her following her ordeal, "the seeds of corruption were in him" (314) on the day that the boy discovered that journal and failed to give it to an adult. Will's obsession with the past is not, then, a matter of reincarnation. It is simply a license he grants himself to act on his own monstrous impulses.

Will Stafford's monstrous impulses raise a secondary theme in *On the Street Where You Live*, the perverse power of the sexual predator. The serial killers and stalkers in the novel, particularly Stafford, Douglas Carter, and Eric Bailey, all have in common the desire to avenge rejection and humiliation by women. In the 1890s, Carter had murdered three young women who rejected his sexual advances. A hundred years later, Will is recreating his great-grandfather's crimes, but not before he has attacked a woman on his own initiative, and Eric Bailey is on the prowl in New York. Years before, after three classmates had refused his invitation to the junior prom, making him the laughingstock of his school, the awkward sixteen-year-old had snapped compromising photographs of Karen Fowler, the girl whose imitation of his inarticulate invitation had caused him the greatest humiliation, and then threatened her with exposure (162–63). Now he is stalking an unsuspecting Emily Graham, who, despite their friendship, feels nothing more than sisterly affection for a man who, despite his superior intellect and expensive wardrobe, still manages to appear "woebegone" (87).

Essentially weak men who need to assert their self-proclaimed superiority, all three discover what Bailey articulates most clearly: "Fear [is] the ultimate weapon of revenge" (184). Holding his evidence against her, Eric Bailey had relished the look in Karen Fowler's eyes when she passed him in the school corridors after the ill-fated prom because "for the first time in his life [he] had felt *powerful*" (163). He gains a similar feeling from the knowledge that Emily's stalker has robbed her of her peace of mind. After all, the woman who destroyed his company and rejected his love should expect nothing more (184). Similarly, Douglas Carter records his "sense of supremacy over his victims" in his diary of death, and his great-grandson, for whom "vicarious sharing" is eventually not enough, soon joins him in "chuckling at his playacting as he grieved with the grieving" (15). To instill terror confirms their belief in their own omnipotence, and thus they compensate for the pain and humiliation of rejection and their own inadequacies.

Yet as Clark's novel makes clear, the sexual predator is little more than a cowardly bully who refuses to confront his weaknesses or take responsibility for his failures. "Rejection," as Eric tells Emily, certainly "can do terrible things to some people" (18). But everyone who experiences the pain of rejection (and that is probably everyone) does not become a serial killer. Emily has herself known betrayal and rejection, but she has mustered her inner resources and moved beyond her hurt (61). Her self-esteem does not depend upon another's suffering, but comes instead from facing hard facts, struggling with failure, and, if necessary, beginning again, as she is doing when she moves to Spring Lake. The sexual predator, in contrast, lacks the courage to change himself. His self-esteem is merely counterfeit, and because he knows it, he must continue his deadly pursuits to maintain his illusion. Should Emily somehow escape death on March 31, she will soon have as much to fear from Eric as she had from Will because stalking is no longer satisfying his need for revenge. He knows that he, too, will have to kill before long (286).

Despite the bleakness of these themes, Clark locates in Spring Lake itself a touchstone of value that makes possible a fundamental belief in humanity—its sense of community. In her memoirs, Phyllis Gates recalled the "palpable" "sadness" that characterized the Spring Lake "community" following Madeline Shapley's disappearance in 1891 (106). A century later, a similar "sense of collective mourning [settles] over the town" (40) following the discovery of the bodies in Emily's backyard. Spring Lake's residents even include their new neighbor in their thoughts. At the memorial service for Martha Lawrence, Carolyn Taylor, a fourth-generation resident of the town, speaks "for *all* of us" when she apologizes to Emily for her distressing situation. "Everyone in this *community*," she tells her, "feels sorry that you've had so much on your plate these last few days" (129).

Clark's use of words such as "collective," "communal," and "community" underscores the common bonds of Spring Lake's citizens, who respond as one to any event in their town. In contrast to the anonymity of life today in most cities no matter their size, neighbors know neighbors in Spring Lake. Those inviting front porches on the city's Victorian houses have never been merely cosmetic features, but rather a symbol of lives shared with others. So the grief of one is the grief of all in Spring Lake. When Madeline Shapley had disappeared in 1891, Phyllis Gates's mother had immediately returned to the resort from her Philadelphia home to comfort the family (89). A century later, Spring Lake's neighbors gather "in quiet dignity" (292) on the pavement at the unearthing of each pair of bodies. In contrast to the intrusive buzz of media helicopters flying overhead, their silent vigil is both a profound acknowledgment of the breach of humanity symbolized by those graves and a heartfelt statement of solidarity against it. Ghoulish curiosity theirs is not.

By the end of *On the Street Where You Live*, Spring Lake's concept of community stands as the novel's positive value. Murder and mayhem can shake but not shatter the foundations of a society that demonstrates compassion for others, that grieves the loss of life, that unites against appalling savagery. Amid such a community, goodness can prevail.

A CULTURAL CRITIQUE OF *ON THE STREET WHERE YOU LIVE*

Clark's emphasis on the concept of community in *On the Street Where You Live*, as well as the contemporary subject of her plot, with its focus on stalkers and serial killers, indicates the degree to which she engages in cultural criticism in her fiction. It provides literary critics who probe a society's cultural artifacts for evidence of its values, attitudes, and behaviors with equally fertile ground for their own analysis. To engage in such cultural criticism is to view the novel as a sociological document that records and reflects the manners and mores of the people who inhabit the world it recreates. Such a perspective looks back to the English poet and critic Matthew Arnold's view that literature offers a critique of life (although Arnold would have disdained the popular fiction that Clark writes). It also bears some connection to Marxist theory, with its emphasis on the material foundation of a culture's ideology. It is not, however, specifically Marxist because it is linked to a tradition of American liberalism concerned not so much with doctrine or methodology but with cultural commentary.

While the field of cultural studies is not new, its recognition as a unique branch of inquiry is a relatively recent development, primarily identified with postmodernism. In other words, it has gained credibility since the end of World War II and indeed has even laid the groundwork for what became the new historicism of the 1980s and 1990s. Cultural critics generally apply the concepts and theories of various disciplines to an examination of the elite arts, popular culture, media, ordinary life, and other aspects of contemporary culture and society. Cultural criticism is, according to Arthur Asa Berger, "a multidisciplinary, interdisciplinary, pandisciplinary, or metadisciplinary undertaking" (2). Consequently, it may involve literary theory, psychoanalytic theory, Marxist theory, and sociological and anthropological theory. Whatever their approach or discipline, however, cultural critics, like new historicists, notes Hans Bertens, "see literary texts as absolutely inseparable from their historical context" (176) and as no different from any other cultural product. "The literary text," observes Bertens, is a "time- and place-bound verbal construction" (177). It is a cultural artifact, in other words, that reveals much about the world that produced it.

Published in 2001, *On the Street Where You Live* would have been written at the millennium, and it is in many ways a typical fin de siècle, or millennial, novel, a form characterized by its apocalyptic presentiments of doom. Straddling two millennia, Clark's novel casts a backward glance with one plot strand and projects another into the dark unknown traditionally associated with a new millennium, offering a somber rumination on both periods. Spring Lake's serial killers are certainly troubling evidence of social breakdown that could herald civilization's end, but two other examples also suggest the debasement of contemporary life. Both highlight an economic system that transforms everything, including human beings, into commodities and thereby devalues all that is meaningful in life.

The first of these examples is the dot-com world of money-for-nothing represented by Eric Bailey. The unprecedented technological revolution of the 1990s, and particularly the development and expansion of the World Wide Web, created the global economy of the last decade of the twentieth century that generated skyrocketing share values on the stock exchange. In such a business climate, every company and every entrepreneur rushed to launch a Web site from which to sell their goods and services, and a universe of dot-com companies, many of which existed only in their inventors' imaginations or lacked the logistics to fulfill their promises, soon sprang into being. Supported by investors who saw profit in their promise, most of these dot-com companies produced spectacular windfalls for their executives and those who invested from the beginning in their success, but by the end of the decade and on the eve of the millennium, they were collapsing just as spectacularly as their failure to deliver the goods exposed their hollowness.

The rise and fall of Eric Bailey's dot-com empire is a prime example of a betrayal of the American ideal of success. Granted, Eric starts with nothing and succeeds by virtue of his ingenuity. But the American ideal is grounded in concepts of hard work and fair play, not on easy money and empty promises. America's great self-made men, its Andrew Carnegies and Henry Fords, were great because they produced something or achieved something, not simply because they invested wisely in the stock market. In the dot-com world of the late twentieth century, however, such men have been replaced by Eric Baileys, the self-made man has been reduced to a confidence man, and an American ideal of rags-to-riches has become little more than grubbing for the almighty dollar. Within this context, it would be hard to muster sympathy for Eric even if he were not a sexual predator. Within this context, he has earned his failure.

The dot-com world of easy money, with its suggestion of economic collapse and the debasement of an American ideal, is one apocalyptic vision of doom in *On the Street Where You Live*. The second is the cult of celebrity embodied in the journalist Reba Ashby and the publication for which she writes, *The National Daily*. At the turn of the twenty-first century, the marriages and divorces of movie stars, the exploits of professional athletes, and even the incredible feats of ordinary people have increasingly substituted for hard news—reports about world events, analyses of government policies, explanations of economic trends—in newspapers and on television. Everybody, as the artist Andy Warhol once observed, wants to be "world famous for fifteen minutes," and publications such as *The Guinness Book of World Records* and television talk shows have created instant celebrities of people who have done nothing more than marry forty-seven times or undergone a sex change. Such stories sell newspapers, increase television ratings, and generate advertising revenue, thereby earning profits for the multinational corporations that increasingly own these news outlets.

The transformation of print and broadcast news into infotainment is a sure sign of the triumph of the commodification of American culture on the eve of the millennium. Celebrity sells: The more famous the face, the more sensational the story, the more the profit. So where once the news was concerned with reporting the story, now it frequently creates it. Journalists vie for the exclusive interview and the tip from the unnamed source, and they swoop down like vultures in the aftermath of human tragedy, shoving a camera and microphone into the face of a grieving parent or spouse. Sometimes, because they can themselves become celebrities, they even hype the angle that will get them the most column inches, the maximum air time. In *On the Street Where You Live*, Reba Ashby is just such a journalist.

From the moment she arrives in Spring Lake, Ashby intends to "milk the story of the reincarnated serial killer for all it was worth" (164). After all, it was her question at the first police news conference that had generated the story (93). For the sake of that story, she attends Dr. Lillian Madden's lecture to ask pointed questions about reincarnation (96–98), thereby fuelling the headlines and inadvertently causing Madden's murder when her questions alert the killer to the psychologist's potential threat to him. She is also an inquisitive "mourner" at the memorial service for Martha Lawrence (165) and descends on Dr. Clayton Wilcox when she learns some incriminating information about him (170–71). Ashby even sinks to pretense when she befriends the septuagenarian Bernice Joyce, who, under the columnist's skillful questioning, reveals confidential information about the Martha Lawrence murder weapon (165–66) and then confides that she may remember seeing someone remove it from the Lawrence house (230–32). When Ashby converts both bits of information into headlines that prompt the killer to strangle the elderly witness, she feels a momentary twinge of guilt that she may have caused yet another murder. But then "her natural instinct for self-protection set in" (270), and she convinces herself that Bernice was responsible for her own murder. For the sake of her story, Reba Ashby can justify any tactic—pretense, insinuation, bribery, and even exposure of personal information—and ignore the very human consequences of her actions—the vicious and unnecessary murders of two innocent women. After all, in a world where the profit margin rules, these two murders and the headlines they produce at least sell newspapers.

Clark's millennial reflections are certainly sobering, for they suggest that American progress and prosperity have come at the expense of human values such as honesty and sincerity and respect for individual life. Her dot-com world of immediate gratification is as shallow as her tabloid world of instant celebrities, which may explain the appeal of Spring Lake's stately and substantial Victorian homes, no matter the complex and very human reality behind their façades, to a modern generation. Her parallel plots, however, challenge that comforting fiction. In fact, the cultural critic might argue that *On the Street Where You Live* makes patently clear that the "reassuring regularity" (39) of life in Spring Lake was as fragile at the turn of the century as it is on the eve of the millennium.

Yet however bleak her millennial reflections, Mary Higgins Clark is not a pessimist. Spring Lake may not be a perfect place, but its concept of community, as she makes clear, is indeed exemplary. Unlike the hordes of journalists who descend on the city to exploit every gory detail of the town's crimes, Spring Lake's residents understand and indeed feel the threat that these murders pose to their peace of mind and way of life and respond appropriately. They share information and work together to restore the order and harmony of their town, and they succeed. What prevails at the end of *On the Street Where You Live* is community—people sharing common bonds of humanity that signify Clark's fundamental belief in our world. In novel after novel, she never loses faith.

11

Daddy's Little Girl
(2002)

Mary Higgins Clark experiments in her 2002 bestseller *Daddy's Little Girl* with a formula that has served her well since the publication of her first novel of suspense more than twenty-five years ago. The result is a poignant examination of murder's living victims that subordinates plot to character to achieve its effect. Certainly *Daddy's Little Girl* has the requisite twists and turns of plot that have made Clark master of her genre, but they create surprisingly little of her trademark suspense in this work. The criminal, after all, has been convicted of and served more than twenty years in prison for the murder of fifteen-year-old Andrea Cavanaugh as the novel begins, so the element of "whodunit," despite Clark's efforts to cast a shadow of suspicion on other suspects, is rarely in doubt. The crime, however, continues to resonate in the lives of those it touched, and Clark makes its legacy her focus in this work by taking readers into the mind of Ellie Cavanaugh, Andrea's younger sister. In her nineteenth novel of suspense, Clark shifts for the first time from a third- to a first-person perspective, a narrative strategy that makes character as compelling as plot.

Daddy's Little Girl is the story of a family destroyed by crime. From the moment seven-year-old Ellie Cavanaugh finds her sister Andrea's battered body in the secret hideaway in which the fifteen-year-old met her friends, her life is never the same. She may have achieved success as an investigative reporter for an Atlanta newspaper, but she lives daily with the memory of Andrea's brutal murder as well as its legacy—her parents' divorce, her "nomadic life" (45) with a mother who turned to alcohol to ease her pain, her estrangement from a father for whom she must have been a poor substitute for his "golden child" (46). So when Robson Parke Westerfield, the handsome scion of a wealthy and prominent family who had been convicted of the crime on the strength of her testimony, comes up for parole, Ellie vows to prevent his release. Twenty-two years in prison, she feels certain, have not redeemed a man who continues to proclaim his innocence of the crime.

Despite Ellie's protests, Westerfield secures his freedom. He and his family then mount a campaign to clear his name by shifting the blame to Paulie Stroebel, a slow-witted classmate who had had a crush on Andrea, and by discrediting Ellie. Fuelled by outrage, Ellie returns to the scene of the crime, Oldham-on-the-Hudson, in New York's Westchester County, to conduct her own investigation into Westerfield's life that will conclusively prove his guilt. Her research leads her to some horrifying truths that compromise her life but that ultimately free her from the grief and guilt that have shadowed her existence.

PLOT

Time shifts mark the three-part structure of *Daddy's Little Girl*, allowing Clark to relate economically events that occur over twenty-five years. Part One details the murder of Andrea Cavanaugh, a pretty and popular flutist in the school band who was secretly dating nineteen-year-old Rob Westerfield in defiance of her father's order to have nothing to do with the spoiled young man who had a reputation as a "troublemaker" (60). In five brief chapters, Clark introduces the novel's central characters and provides two possible suspects for the murder. Most important, she dramatizes the key events that will make this murder the defining reality of Ellie Cavanaugh's life. Not only will the seven-year-old discover her sister's body, but she will also overhear conversations that begin with the phrase "If only Ellie . . . " (21–22) and witness her father's inconsolable grief as, clutching a photo of his beloved daughter, he sobs in accompaniment to the tune "Daddy's Little Girl" that drifts from the music box he had lovingly presented to his firstborn. Those memories will haunt Ellie into adulthood.

Part Two of *Daddy's Little Girl*, which brings readers to its contemporary setting and constitutes the bulk of the novel, is essentially two stories. The first story reveals the truth about Andrea Cavanaugh's murder; the second discloses that murder's effect on the Cavanaugh family, particularly on Ellie. Clark's shift to the first-person point of view in this section indicates that both stories are equally important.

The first story is vintage Clark. Twenty-three years after Andrea's murder, on the eve of a third parole hearing that seems certain this time to result in Rob Westerfield's release from prison, Ellie Cavanaugh returns to Oldham-on-the-Hudson, New York, determined to prevent its happening. Her failure and the Westerfields' efforts to secure a new trial for the heir to the family name set in motion a series of events that includes threats, intimidation, and two attempts on Ellie's life. Undeterred by the danger she faces, Ellie investigates every aspect of Rob Westerfield's life, questioning reluctant witnesses and revealing criminal behavior that the Westerfield fortune and influence have managed to conceal. Although Ellie never swerves from her belief in Westerfield's guilt, she does discover information about both Paulie Stroebel and Will Nebels, the handyman originally questioned in Andrea's murder who now comes forward to incriminate Stroebel, that could challenge her memory of the crime and that Clark certainly intends to cast doubt in readers' minds. The first-person point of view from which she writes this section of the novel, however, undermines this effort. So strong is Ellie's conviction, so strong are readers' understanding of and identification with Ellie's thoughts and sensibility, that any doubt about Westerfield's guilt is fleeting. Her final confrontation with the killer simply confirms what Ellie and readers have known all along. In typical fashion, Clark brings her tale of secrets and suspense to an emotionally satisfying conclusion.

The second story also has elements of Clark's signature style, for she has always to some extent probed character in her fiction. Nancy Harmon, for instance, the heroine of her first novel, *Where Are the Children?* (1975), must overcome issues of identity if she is to rescue her children from the psychopath who intends to destroy them all, and the discovery of her father's secret life in *I'll Be Seeing You* (1993) prompts Meghan Collins to similar self-examination. Indeed, their confrontations with crime lead virtually all of Clark's heroines to personal growth and a heightened sense of self. In *Daddy's Little Girl*, however, what is usually a secondary element in her novel, this story of personal growth, becomes a primary focus. Clark signals its importance in her use of the first-person point of view. In effect, that point of view makes the central drama of *Daddy's Little Girl* Ellie's triumph over the grief and guilt that have defined her life.

The novel's final chapter, set one year after Ellie's mission, functions as an epilogue that brings satisfying closure to Clark's two tales. Readers discover the fate of Rob Westerfield, of course, but more important, they see evidence that Ellie is finally at peace. Her marriage to Pete Lawlor, her reconciliation with her father, her friendship with her half-brother and stepmother all give promise of the happiness Ellie deserves. The epilogue's focus on Ellie's life makes clear that her story is indeed the heart of *Daddy's Little Girl.*

POINT OF VIEW

Clark's use of the first-person point of view, or perspective from which readers see the action, is, as previously noted, crucial to the development of *Daddy's Little Girl.* It marks a development in Clark's style as well. All of her previous novels have had a third-person narrator, an omniscient voice capable of relating events past and present as well as the thoughts and feelings of any number of characters. The narrative strategy has allowed Clark to shift from scene to scene, from character to character, withholding some information from her heroines but providing it to her readers and thus creating her novels' suspense. From their privileged perspective, readers know the dangers that threaten Clark's heroines but are powerless to act on their knowledge. On the brief occasions when Clark has delivered chapters of her narratives from the first-person point of view, she always limits that perspective to the criminal mind. The result, as readers of *Stillwatch* (1984), *Loves Music, Loves to Dance* (1991), *On the Street Where You Live* (2001) as well as several other Clark classics can attest, is a chilling depiction of obsession, megalomania, amorality, paranoia, indeed of all the perverse states of mind and being that explain criminal behavior. That glimpse into the criminal mind is yet another strategy by which Clark creates and maintains suspense.

Clark's shift to the first-person point of view, or "I" perspective, in *Daddy's Little Girl* signals her intention to write something different from her typical novel of suspense. One of the first consequences of her narrative strategy, in fact, is to diminish the novel's suspense. Because readers see and know only what Ellie experiences and thinks, they no longer possess special knowledge that fills them with dread as they anticipate some inevitable horror. They do not live in fear of either the fire or the automobile chase, in other words, that nearly takes Ellie's life because, like the novel's heroine, they do not know that such danger threatens until it occurs.

Another consequence of Clark's strategy is to diminish the element of mystery in the novel. A third-person point of view has been one of the conventions, or standard features, of the mystery since the genre's development because it delays revelation of the criminal's identity and thus provides readers with equal opportunity as the investigator to solve the crime. In fact, it even makes it possible to match wits with the investigator and perhaps to solve the crime before that superior mind does. A first-person point of view, however, eliminates the element of "whodunit" by its simultaneous revelation of crucial evidence to both the investigator and the reader, which is exactly the case in *Daddy's Little Girl*. Despite Clark's efforts to divert suspicion to both Paulie Stroebel and Will Nebels, readers remain unconvinced. Readers have little doubt, in fact, of Rob Westerfield's guilt because they know what Ellie knows and see what Ellie sees. They trust Ellie's perceptions, moreover, and in consequence accept her truths.

Mystery and suspense may have been sacrificed by Clark's shift to a first-person point of view in *Daddy's Little Girl*, but in their place is an increased emphasis on character and, as a corollary, theme. Indeed, that first-person point of view, which by convention makes the "I" narrator the focus of the literary work, indicates that Clark's purpose in this novel is to dramatize one woman's efforts to reclaim her life after her sister's murder has destroyed all that she remembers as good in it. Her challenge, of course, is to make this story of personal growth and change as compelling as her tale of crime and punishment. Here, again, Clark's narrative strategy works for her. The first-person point of view leads readers to identify with Ellie Cavanaugh. They understand her guilt, empathize with her grief, and share her desires because they experience her thoughts and sensibility more intimately than they would if a third-person narrator merely related them. In the end, Ellie Cavanaugh is a real presence in *Daddy's Little Girl* and a worthy substitute for twists and turns of plot.

CHARACTER DEVELOPMENT

Gabrielle "Ellie" Cavanaugh, a thirty-year-old investigative reporter with the *Atlanta News*, may possess all the qualities of a typical Clark heroine, but Clark's presentation of those qualities is anything but typical in *Daddy's Little Girl*. Forthright and determined, resilient and resourceful, sensitive and intelligent, Ellie is without doubt Clark's embodiment of good in the novel. But she is not a stereotype because Clark's narrative strategy reveals her doubts and fears, her hopes and dreams, and, above all, the grief and guilt that have defined her life since the day she discovered her sister's battered body. Acutely self-aware, Ellie admits to arrogance, acknowledging that "When I think I'm right, all the forces of heaven and hell won't budge me" and likening herself and her efforts to prove Rob Westerfield's guilt to the literary hero Don Quixote's "tilting at windmills" (140). She understands what her obsession is doing to her life and does not want it to happen, but seems powerless to give it up (85). Ellie Cavanaugh is clearly a complex character, and Clark presents her in all her complexity.

The brief glimpse of seven-year-old Ellie that Clark provides in Part One of the novel offers key insights into her adult self and, most important, delineates the family relationships that will shape her life. Even at seven years, for instance, Ellie was instinctively aware that Andrea, their father's "golden child" (46), was the family's center. Pretty and feminine, Andrea resembled their mother, Genine, whereas Ellie was developing already the strong features of their father, Ted. Popular and vivacious, Andrea enjoyed a laugh, even if her antics resulted in reprimand, but nobody seemed to mind. In fact, it was impossible for anyone not to love her, and Ellie certainly did. Entrusted with her teenage idol's secrets, including her crush on Rob Westerfield, his gift of an engraved locket that she wore hidden beneath her clothing, and the hideaway in his grandmother's garage where she met him and her friends to sneak a cigarette and talk, Ellie was thrilled to be included in her life and especially proud that her sister considered her a "good kid." "She's not a snitch," Andrea would boast to her friends when she brought Ellie to their hideout (6). Ellie's trustworthiness and her desire to please her sister will eventually be a source of one of the "If onlys" that shadow her life. "If only," she frets, she had told all she knew, Andrea might still be alive. Certainly that is the implication of the observation she overhears Mrs. Lewis, one of her mother's friends, make (21–22). It is the implication as well of the question her father puts to her following her discovery of her sister's body: "Why didn't you *tell* us . . . " that you knew where Andrea may have gone? (12). Guilt and blame attach themselves to Ellie from that point in her life.

Her father's question, of course, is most damaging to the bewildered and aching child because it reinforces Ellie's vague understanding that she will be an inadequate replacement for her elder sister. Although at seven years Ellie had been too young for jealousy to flower into sibling rivalry, its seeds were germinating. Andrea, after all, had been "Daddy's little girl." At her birth, their father had given her a music box that played their special song as well as a silver picture frame engraved with that special phrase. When Ellie asked whether her father had danced her to sleep as he had Andrea, her mother replied "no": Ellie was "always a good sleeper" and had been "no trouble at all" (22). Such a response must surely have sounded like disregard or neglect to a child, especially a child whose question betrayed her desire to be "daddy's little girl" as well. Ellie adored her father, too, and was "in awe," she remembers, of the man who, "[she] bragged to [herself] saved people's lives" (50). Yet her father seemed never to notice. When she intruded, therefore, on his private grief, she simply retreated from the scene, instinctively aware that she could never adequately comfort him (22). Years later, Ellie will recall that afternoon, with its indelible image of "the father I worshiped, sobbing and hugging my dead sister's picture against his chest" to the "fragile sounds" of "Daddy's Little Girl" that drifted from the music box, as "the defining day of my life" (33). Further proof of her insignificance was unnecessary.

Through the passing years, however, Ellie finds that proof, and neither her mother nor her father is blameless for contributing to their daughter's hurt, guilt, and sense of abandonment. A "flash of memory," for instance, reminds Ellie that she had once complained to her mother that the wallpaper in her bedroom, with its "little-girl cutesy, . . . Cinderella-motif," was "babyish." Her mother replied that it was nearly a duplicate of the paper that had covered Andrea's bedroom walls when she was Ellie's age and that "*She* loved it" (153), failing to recognize in the complaint Ellie's desire to be recognized and appreciated for herself, a fact that clearly did not escape the young child. Similarly, upon her death, her mother's most significant legacy to Ellie was a "bulky suitcase" containing the newspaper clippings and the trial transcript relating to Andrea's murder. This "Pandora's box of misery" which was, Ellie believes, her mother's "private crucifixion" (72), simply adds to the baggage of guilt and grief that the young woman already carries.

Her parents' divorce shortly after Andrea's murder, however, is certainly the most compelling evidence of Ellie's insignificance because it suggests that neither cared enough about their surviving daughter to meet her needs. With her mother, who descended into alcoholism during her years working as a "troubleshooter" for a national hotel chain, Ellie embarked on a "nomadic life" (45), moving from one hotel to another in city after city. Such a life denied her the reassuring sense of stability that comes of taking root in a community and the comforting satisfaction that results from lasting friendships. During these years, Ellie's father, who had remarried three years after his divorce, diligently posted his support check each month, but from Ellie's perspective, "whatever he felt for me was not enough to make him desire my presence" (46–47). Adoration gradually changed from hurt to resentment as Ellie realized that the dream she had nurtured even before Andrea's death—that when her sister went off to college her father would notice her and give her "the attention I craved from him" (47)—would never come true. Locked in their private misery, Ted and Genine Cavanaugh were simply unable to recognize the harm they had done their daughter, however unintentionally it occurred. By the time Ellie reaches adulthood, she has "lived with the memory" of Andrea's "brutal murder" all her life (64). Indeed, that memory has become her life and has made it little more than an existence.

Ellie Cavanaugh's determination to prove Rob Westerfield's culpability thus lies in her own unresolved grief and guilt. It springs as well from her desire to reclaim her life. Uncovering the evidence of Westerfield's vicious criminality, including his murder of Amy Rayburn just months before he killed Andrea, returns him to prison for life and allows Ellie to pay the debt she feels she owes her sister and is, in fact (and despite the attempts on her life), her easiest task. Reclaiming her life, however, is more difficult because it involves an honest appraisal of the past, chiefly as it relates to her father, that challenges Ellie's memory of events and demands consideration of an alternate version of her story. Ellie's confrontation with her half-brother Teddy will force her to that reappraisal.

When Ellie lies in the hospital following the first attempt on her life, she and her father, a retired state trooper, meet for the first time in nearly twenty years, and that process of reappraisal begins. Ellie, however, is not yet willing to forgive her father, nor is she willing to admit any complicity in their estrangement. To her thinly veiled accusation of abandonment, for example, he reminds her, "You refused to visit me" (166). To her cruel observation that he was the cause of her mother's death, he painfully observes, "Ellie, your mother left me" (167). Throughout their brief meeting, Ellie returns her father's genuine concern for her safety with snide remarks and hurtful accusations that are intended to demonstrate her lack of attachment and self-sufficiency, but actually betray her heartache and need of him. Yet her father cannot breach her defensive barriers. In some perverse way, Ellie still prefers to spend her life "yearning for what [she] had lost" (248) rather than accepting what she could have had and what she still can have, and she still holds her father responsible for her losses. It will take her father's surrogate, her half-brother Teddy, to succeed where the elder man fails.

The seventeen-year-old basketball star who resembles their father, and thus Ellie, in every way, including the flash of his eyes when roused (252), is clearly Ted Cavanaugh's substitute. He voices his father's pain and regret, his guilt about Andrea's murder (254), and, most important, his fear that he is going to lose his other "little girl" (255). From Teddy, Ellie learns that her father had secretly attended her college graduation, that he had subscribed to the *Atlanta News* to read her columns, that he had never stopped talking about or caring for her (253). In fact, Teddy's pride in the half-sister he has never known (201) is simply the expression of their father's. Because Ellie will not be "rude" to this earnest young man (200) (and perhaps because at some level she wants to listen to what he has to say), she does hear her father's version of their story, and like the obituary that her father had printed at her mother's death, it begins to change her perception of the past. In fact, it leads to the self-examination essential to reclaiming her life.

Following Teddy's second visit, Ellie seriously probes her memory of the past, particularly her assumption of all the guilt for Andrea's murder, and asks a crucial question: "Did the three of us *choose* to harbor guilt and grief within our own souls?" (254). To what extent, in other words, were they complicit for their own suffering and responsible for their own failures? Her answer, when it comes, is both distressing and liberating. Wrapped in the mantle of her grief and guilt, Ellie admits to herself, she had reason to be selfish, and she was (271). Her parents' pain, by implication, must have been equally destructive. They had all in effect failed each other when they most needed each other. With this understanding, Ellie can finally begin to forgive her parents and, most important, herself. With this understanding, she can also embrace the future and begin a life of her own.

Foreshadowing Ellie's triumph over guilt and grief is the restoration of her religious faith, another victim of Andrea's murder. When Ellie recalls her happy past, it includes Sunday drives to Graymoor, a Franciscan monastery and retreat house, where the Cavanaugh family would attend Mass, followed by brunch at the Bear Mountain Inn. In the years following Andrea's murder, however, and her mother's death, Ellie had turned from her faith. On the obligatory occasions such as Christmas and Easter when she attended Mass, her heart was not in her words, and she had no praise to sing (92). God, after all, had failed her. He had not answered her petition to return Andrea to them (227). Ellie's anger at this failure had eventually dissolved into weariness (92) and emptiness. But as she holds vigil following Paulie Stroebel's suicide attempt, Ellie finds herself praying, instinctively at first, but then consciously, not only for Paulie's recovery, but also for acceptance of God's will (178). Days later, Ellie makes a deliberate detour at Graymoor to recapture a slowly surfacing memory of her last visit, when she asked the impossible of God. Reduced to tears by the memory, she unburdens her feelings to a sympathetic priest, who helps her to recover her faith (227). The peace of mind and soul that Ellie finds in her reconciliation with God gives promise of the happiness that awaits her after she exorcises her demons and lays to rest the unquiet spirits that have haunted her existence. That certainly seems Clark's point in setting her novel's contemporary beginning at Halloween, the date of Rob Westerfield's parole from prison (69), and evoking the religious significance of All Saints Day and its restoration of order.

Ellie Cavanaugh is one of Clark's most complex characters, and the novel's narrative strategy, its first-person point of view, discloses all the strengths and weaknesses of her being. That same strategy, however, limits to her perceptions of them the representation of its secondary characters, whose thoughts and feelings readers cannot know unless the characters speak them to or enact them before Ellie. In consequence, the secondary characters in *Daddy's Little Girl*, including suspects Paulie Stroebel and Will Nebels, retired detective Marcus Longo, and Andrea's former best friend Joan Lashley St. Martin, are little more than vehicles by which to advance the plot. Clark certainly gives them sufficient background and personal detail to establish their reality, but their essential selves are unimportant to Ellie's quest and thus unexplored. Even Ted Cavanaugh, whose own guilt and grief must be as profound as his daughter's is, remains essentially an enigma. Readers, for instance, who, like Ellie, must surely want to know his reasons for not fighting to save his family by pursuing his wife and daughter to Florida (167), never get sufficient answer, so it is hard to know and to evaluate his character. These secondary characters are clearly not Clark's focus. In fact, among them, only her criminal, Rob Westerfield, earns more than cursory character development, and then, like the typical Clark villain, he is essentially a stereotype.

As Craig Parshall, a spokesperson for Arbinger Preparatory School, from which Rob departed his studies after less than two years, explains to Ellie, Westerfield is a "sociopath" (108), born without conscience, without compassion, completely amoral and incapable of adapting to the established moral code. Such clinical explanation easily disposes of any need to explore Westerfield's motivation for criminal behavior. Instead of analysis, Clark substitutes a litany of Westerfield's offenses—his drug problem (212), his abuse of a teenage waitress (111–13), his attack on a rival for a starting position on Arbinger's football team (108), his plot to have his grandmother murdered to secure her $100,000 bequest (211–16), all of which culminate in his murders of Amy Rayburn and Andrea Cavanaugh.

Westerfield is clearly more than the "troublemaker" (60) many considered him to be. He is, as his name indicates, someone who robs the innocent of life and, for survivors like Ellie, life of meaning. He is, as his alias, Jim Wilding, suggests, a predatory "beast" (35) with killer instincts. In fact, Clark emphasizes this aspect of his character by her use of an animal metaphor. Westerfield's "animal magnetism," for instance, indicates to Ellie the "strength and confidence that is the trademark of many powerful men" (141), and she fears what he will do when he is "uncaged" (64; 84). Others confirm her perceptions by stating boldly that he is an "animal" (112; 190). Clark, without doubt, would concur with this assessment. Like all of her criminals, Rob Westerfield, who has nothing to redeem him, deserves his punishment.

THEMATIC DEVELOPMENT

In her depiction of Ellie Cavanaugh's grief and guilt, Clark grounds the major theme of *Daddy's Little Girl,* for it is a novel that explores the repercussions of violence on the lives of those it touches. At the center of this analysis, of course, are the Cavanaughs. Andrea Cavanaugh's murder initiates a series of reactions and responses that effectively destroys her family, both individually and collectively. Robbed by her sister's murder of both the life she had and the life she might have had, Ellie grows into adulthood calling an existence a life and spending much of that existence regretfully contemplating "if onlys" and "what might have beens." Tormented by guilt over his inability to protect his daughter, Ted Cavanaugh, a state trooper, finds himself paralyzed into inaction when his wife Genine walks away from their marriage shortly after their tragedy, taking Ellie with her. Her efforts to escape her grief, however, cannot prevent her from descending into alcoholism, an illness that kills her in middle age. Andrea was clearly not Rob Westerfield's only victim.

The Cavanaughs may lie at the center of *Daddy's Little Girl'*s thematic issues, but as Ellie's investigations unearth Westerfield's buried past, Clark compounds the evidence that proves her point. Christopher Cassidy, for instance, suffered a broken nose and jaw in an unprovoked attack when Westerfield lost to him the starting position as running back on Arbinger Prep's football team (189), and Margaret Fisher still remembers the verbal abuse and twisted arm she suffered when Westerfield, during an argument with his father, jumped up from the table and backed into a serving tray she was carrying, causing the food to spill over him (111–12). Even his grandmother, whose murder he plotted, is not immune to his cruelty. In fact, the heart attack that eventually kills her is most certainly precipitated by the evidence of his complicity in the crime that Ellie puts on her Web site (266). The subplots about Paulie Stroebel and Amy Rayburn, however, provide the best supporting evidence of Clark's central point that violence, especially murder, makes victims of the living as well as the dead.

Twenty-two years in prison do not, of course, change Rob Westerfield's essential nature, so his efforts to frame Paulie Stroebel for Andrea's murder and thereby exonerate himself are hardly surprising. Neither is the result of those efforts. An unequal opponent, Paulie, for whom earnest plodding substitutes for intellectual cleverness, cannot bear to be accused of murdering the classmate he adored. He also fears that he will accidentally disclose information about the crime that he withheld at his mother's advice during the initial investigation, an act that some might construe as evidence of guilt. Unable to cope with his feelings and with limited understanding of his situation, Paulie slashes his wrists in a suicide attempt that nearly succeeds. Had Paulie succeeded, Westerfield would certainly have been guilty of manslaughter in the death.

Westerfield's murder of Amy Rayburn, a crime for which another man, Dan Mayotte, had been wrongly convicted, serves as a sad parallel to the Cavanaugh case and as such provides the most compelling reinforcement of Clark's theme. Like Andrea, Amy was a vivacious teenager when Westerfield, apparently for the thrill of killing, bludgeoned her to death barely six months before Andrea suffered the same fate. When Ellie interviews them, the Rayburns confess to "living [the] nightmare" (276) of their only child's murder ever since, just as the Cavanaughs have been doing. Every detail is as vivid to them as if the event occurred the preceding day. They tell her as well about Dan Mayotte, who served eighteen years in prison for the crime, where, "instead of at Yale" (278), he earned his college degree, and about Mayotte's mother. His conviction "broke [her] heart" (279), they reveal, and probably contributed to her early death. When Ellie concludes her interview with the Rayburns, she totes up the victims of Westerfield's crimes and is "enraged" (279) by the number. Clark's readers should be as well.

Mayotte's fate is the central irony, or reversal, in *Daddy's Little Girl*, and it, too, reinforces Clark's theme. For twenty-three years, Rob Westerfield has maintained his innocence of Andrea's murder and claimed that he has been the victim of a miscarriage of justice. For twenty-three years, of course, a miscarriage of justice has occurred, but it was Mayotte, not Westerfield, who was wronged. Westerfield, in fact, has only ever left a trail of innocent victims, both living and dead, on his life's journey. His living legacy of sorrow and blame, blight and destruction is the troubling heart of *Daddy's Little Girl*.

A MARXIST READING OF *DADDY'S LITTLE GIRL*

Heir to an illustrious name and a comfortable fortune, Robson Parke Westerfield embodies the power, prestige, and privilege of America's upper class. His victims, in contrast, nearly all represent the middle and working classes. This difference in material and social standing offers the Marxist critic, who examines literature from the perspective of class consciousness and class conflict, as outlined in chapter 5, with some compelling evidence of profound inequities in American society and its institutions. Such inequities provide some explanation for Rob Westerfield's behavior. They also suggest an alternate interpretation of the significance of Andrea Cavanaugh's murder. From a Marxist perspective, in fact, *Daddy's Little Girl* is a cautionary tale about social climbing that makes Andrea the victim of her and her mother's misdirected aspirations.

Rob Westerfield may indeed be a sociopath, but he is also a child of privilege with a deeply ingrained sense of entitlement. He has grown into adulthood, after all, in expectation of inheriting a fortune and understanding everything that fortune can buy. He need not place his discarded clothing in a hamper or hang it in the closet—Rosita, the maid, will do it for him (19). He need not worry if he attacks a fellow student—his family's ability to hire lawyers and to compensate victims will protect him from the consequences of his crimes. Besides, people like Rosita and Margaret Fisher, the waitress at The Library, Paulie Stroebel, and Christopher Cassidy, the "son of a short-order cook" (1990) on scholarship to Arbinger Preparatory, people, in other words, who belong to the working class, are inconsequential—unless, of course, they can be useful, like Alfie and Skip Leeds, whom Rob had once hired to murder his grandmother.

Rob may have learned to conceal his "condescending sneer" (86) during his years of imprisonment, but he is still vicious and manipulative and intelligent enough to continue to use the Westerfield reputation to his advantage on his release. When his family launches the Web site intended to restore his reputation, it displays pictures of Rob with his grandfather, a United States senator, of Rob assisting his grandmother at the opening of a Westerfield children's center, of Rob setting off with his parents aboard the *Queen Elizabeth II*, of Rob "dressed in tennis whites at The Everglades Club" (203). These images, which transform the Westerfields into "American royalty," are, Ellie realizes, clearly intended to convey the point that "it was beneath the dignity of this privileged young man to take a human life" (203).

Family and fortune do not, however, signify individual worth. Westerfield's great-grandfather may have been governor of New York, his grandfather may have been a member of Congress, but his father is a "robber baron" (80), a ruthless property developer who would build "a shopping mall in the middle of the Hudson River" if he could get it zoned for business use (81). And Rob, of course, is a murderer. Nor does a private education at exclusive preparatory schools signify human value. Certainly such schools develop men as worthy as previous generations of Westerfields as well as a Christopher Cassidy. But for the price of a renovated athletic center (241) or a refurbished science hall (107), after all, a Carrington Academy or an Arbinger School will nurture a killer.

The ugly truth about class is the assumptions it leads people to make about others—and even about themselves—based on extrinsic factors rather than intrinsic qualities. Alfie Leeds at least tries to redeem himself by assisting Ellie's investigations, whereas Westerfield never admits his guilt. Even Alfie, however, might have difficulty recognizing his moral superiority in the face of Westerfield's social and financial status. Genine Cavanaugh makes a similar error. She confuses the appearance of respectability with its reality, and her daughter Andrea pays the price.

Genine Cavanuagh clearly intended that she and her family should rise on the social scale. Behind the Cavanaugh move from their comfortable home in Irvington, where Ted had been raised and which he never wanted to leave, to their new home in Westchester County two years before Andrea's murder, was Genine's desire for "a bigger house and more property" (6), one sign of her social aspirations. Although Ted never felt comfortable in their new community (and returned to Irvington when his marriage collapsed), Genine quickly set about establishing herself in all the right organizations. She joined the bridge club and the Women's Club, of which both Rob's grandmother and his mother were members (40), and determined "to cultivate a garden" that would be a showpiece of the Oldham Garden Club spring tour (66). From the time they settled in Oldham, moreover, Genine began to train her daughters in formal etiquette because she wanted them *"to know how to do things nicely. . . . That way,"* she had told Ellie, *"if you met someone with a very good background, you'd be able to hold your own"* (105). She insisted that the family eat dinner each evening in the dining room and that they set the table with silver and china for Sunday luncheon (14). She also took her daughters antiques hunting so that they would develop *"an eye for lovely things"* (78). Acutely aware of class distinctions, she even instructed Ellie that expressions of thanks for waiter or waitress service were unnecessary and inappropriate (141).

Aware of the Westerfield cachet, Genine, as Ellie recalls, may not have been as opposed as her husband was to Andrea's relationship with Rob (40). In fact, at their daughter's wake, her husband virtually accuses her of complicity in Andrea's murder because she could not see behind the façade of the Westerfield image. When Dorothy Westerfield arrives to pay her condolences to the family, Ted orders her from their home and accuses her grandson of the crime. Utterly humiliated, Genine begins to apologize for her husband's outburst, but he cuts her short, refusing to let her grovel for Westerfield forgiveness. During their subsequent argument, each faults the other for failing to protect their daughter, and Ted's bitter observation, "If you had not been kissing the hand of anyone named Westerfield—" (43), certainly contains an essence of truth. Genine Cavanaugh craved the Westerfield life, or at least what she perceived as the Westerfield life, with its vast estates and imposing mansion, its ease and grace and dignity, and she wanted it for her daughters, as Andrea certainly knew.

On those Sundays when Andrea set the table with silver and china, her joke that "Lord Malcolm Bigbottom" would be joining them for luncheon (14–15) expressed an understanding of the class distinctions inherent in her mother's lessons. While her amusement may have indicated disdain for those distinctions, she could not have been immune to them. She must have been aware of her mother's reverence for the Westerfields, for as Joan Lashley St. Martin, Andrea's teenage friend, tells Ellie, "your mother had talked a lot about how important the Westerfield family was" (135). She must, therefore, at least initially, have been flattered by Rob Westerfield's attention. She was certainly willing to disobey her father to see him. Andrea may, in fact, have been more her mother's daughter, as their physical resemblance and similar tastes attest, than her "daddy's little girl." She may, in other words, have been as infatuated with and desirous of the Westerfield life as Genine was.

From this perspective, which certainly reveals its grounding in a Marxist ideology of class consciousness and class conflict, Rob Westerfield's murder of Andrea Cavanaugh sounds a clear warning. Andrea had stepped beyond the bounds of her station. For her trespass, which threatened the status quo, she must be killed. The Westerfield world is, in effect, a closed system. It sustains itself on its expensive preparatory schools, its exclusive clubs, and its distinguished reputations. It may occasionally admit a Christopher Cassidy to its ivied halls, but it will never let him forget, as Rob Westerfield's attack makes clear, that he does not belong there. Americans may like to believe that theirs is a democratic system that gives every person equal opportunity to rise to the top, but Andrea's fate suggests otherwise. Class distinctions create some insurmountable social barriers. Andrea simply fell victim to them.

A Marxist reading of *Daddy's Little Girl* exposes the false assumptions about the value of the upper classes that can lead to pervasive discontent and self-destruction. The Westerfields are clearly no better than the Cavanaughs. They simply have more money, and that money buys them power and influence and a standard of living not necessarily related to their talents and achievements and certainly not indicative of their worth. Ellie, who, as the novel's central character, also provides the authorial perspective, instinctively understands this truth. Despite her mother's admonishment, she believes courtesy is never inappropriate and could not imagine failing to extend it to anyone, whatever his or her circumstance, who has earned it (141). In disinheriting both her son and her grandson (266; 269), Dorothy Westerfield testifies to a similar understanding. To be worthy of respectability, she must earn it. Class distinctions merely obscure our common humanity.

Clark may have experimented with a formula in *Daddy's Little Girl*, but her vision is clearly as humane as ever. In fact, her narrative strategy may actually emphasize its humanity. Ellie Cavanaugh is the novel's touchstone of value. She speaks from experience and with conviction of the pain of loss, the guilt of survival, and she has a firm sense of truth and justice. By allowing Ellie to voice her thoughts and feelings directly to readers in a first-person narrative rather than through the mediation of an objective narrator, Clark gives increased authority to her view, and because Ellie is the voice of her creator, Clark achieves the same benefit. In *Daddy's Little Girl*, Clark's advocacy of traditional human values, her outrage at crime, and her faith in an ordered world where right eventually prevails receive their clearest sounding yet.

Bibliography

Page numbers in the text refer to the paperback editions of Mary Higgins Clark's novels, with the exception of the following: *Daddy's Little Girl, Deck the Halls, He Sees You When You're Sleeping, On the Street Where You Live, Silent Night,* and *You Belong to Me.* Page numbers for these books refer to the hardcover editions.

WORKS BY MARY HIGGINS CLARK

All Around the Town. New York: Simon and Schuster, 1992; Pocket Books, 1993.

All Through the Night: A Suspense Story. New York: Simon and Schuster, 1998; Pocket Books, 1999.

"All-Star Trees." *Good Housekeeping,* December 1995: 89–90.

"Always a Storyteller." *The Writer,* August 1987: 9–11.

The Anastasia Syndrome and Other Stories. New York: Simon and Schuster, 1989; Pocket Books, 1991.

Aspire to the Heavens: A Portrait of George Washington. New York: Meredith Press, 1969.

Before I Say Good-Bye. New York: Simon and Schuster, 2000; Pocket Books, 2001.

The Cradle Will Fall. New York: Simon and Schuster, 1980; Pocket Books, 1991.

A Cry in the Night. New York: Simon and Schuster, 1982; Pocket Books, 1993.

Daddy's Little Girl. New York: Simon and Schuster, 2002; Pocket Books, 2003.

Deck the Halls. With Carol Higgins Clark. New York: Simon and Schuster, 2000; Pocket Books, 2001.

He Sees You When You're Sleeping: A Novel. With Carol Higgins Clark. New York: Simon and Schuster, 2001; Pocket Books, 2002.

I'll Be Seeing You. New York: Simon and Schuster, 1993; Pocket Books, 1994.

Kitchen Privileges: A Memoir. New York: Simon and Schuster, 2002.

Let Me Call You Sweetheart. New York: Simon and Schuster, 1995; Pocket Books, 1996.

The Lottery Winner: Alvirah and Willy Stories. New York: Simon and Schuster, 1994; Pocket Books, 1995.

Loves Music, Loves to Dance. New York: Simon and Schuster, 1991; Pocket Books, 1992.

Moonlight Becomes You. New York: Simon and Schuster, 1996; Pocket Books, 1997.

Mount Vernon Love Story: A Novel of George and Martha Washington. New York: Simon and Schuster, 2002; Pocket Books, 2003.

My Gal Sunday. New York: Simon and Schuster, 1996; Pocket Books, 1997.

On the Street Where You Live. New York: Simon and Schuster, 2001; Pocket Books, 2002.

Pretend You Don't See Her. New York: Simon and Schuster, 1997; Pocket Books, 1998.

Remember Me. New York: Simon and Schuster, 1994; Pocket Books, 1995.

Silent Night. New York: Simon and Schuster, 1995; Pocket Books, 1996.

Stillwatch. New York: Simon and Schuster, 1984; Dell, 1988.

A Stranger Is Watching. New York: Simon and Schuster, 1978; Dell, 1988.

"Suspense Writing." *The Writer,* September 1980: 9–12.

"Taking the Plunge," *The Writer,* July 1992: 5–6.

Weep No More, My Lady. New York: Simon and Schuster, 1987; Dell, 1988.

We'll Meet Again. New York: Simon and Schuster, 1999; Pocket Books, 2000.

Where Are the Children? New York: Simon and Schuster, 1975; Pocket Books, 1992.

While My Pretty One Sleeps. New York: Simon and Schuster, 1989; Pocket Books, 1990.

You Belong to Me. New York: Simon and Schuster, 1998; Pocket Books, 1999.

WORKS ABOUT MARY HIGGINS CLARK

Brady, Lois Smith. "Mary Higgins Clark, John Conheeney." *New York Times,* 8 December 1996: L69.

Coiner, Jill Brooke. "She Dunnit!" *Family Circle,* 22 December 1992: 60–63.

Conroy, Sarah Booth. "The Family Plots." *Washington Post,* 28 September 1993: C1, C4.

Donohue, John W. "Of Many Things." *America,* 1 May 1993: 2.

Fakih, Kimberly Olson. "The Reassuring Triumph of the Good: An Interview with Mary Higgins Clark." *Library Journal,* 15 March 1990: 35–37.

Freeman, Lucy. "Mary Higgins Clark." *Armchair Detective* 18, 3(1985): 228–37.

Hoch, Edward D. "Clark, Mary Higgins." In *Twentieth Century Crime and Mystery Writers*. 3rd ed. Ed. Lesley Henderson. Chicago: St. James, 1991: 210–11.

Hoopes, Roy. "Shedunnit." *Modern Maturity*, August–September 1989: 52–57.

Hubbard, Kim, and Liz McNeil. "Once More, with Feeling." *People*, 16 December 1996. EBSCOhost. On-line. 29 January 2001.

Kopecky, Gini. "The Way We Were." *Redbook*, March 1991: 101–8.

Kuczynski, Alex. "Updating a Paperback Heroine." *The New York Times*, 22 May 2000: C1, C17.

Lipton, Michael A., and Ann Guerin. "Murders, They Write." *People*, 2 November 1992: 79–82.

"Mary Higgins Clark." *U. S. News & World Report*, 26 October 1992: 32.

"Mary Higgins Clark & John Conheeney." *People*, 10 February 1997: 80.

Mitgang, Herbert. "Mary Higgins Clark." *New York Times Book Review*, 14 May 1978: 52.

O'Brien, Maureen. "Mary Higgins Clark Lands $35 Million Deal with S & S." *Publishers Weekly*, 19 October 1992: 9.

O'Neill, Elizabeth Hill. "PW Interviews: Mary Higgins Clark." *Publisher's Weekly*, 19 May 1989: 64–65.

Pelzer, Linda C. *Mary Higgins Clark: A Critical Companion*. Westport, Conn: Greenwood Press, 1995.

"Pen Pals for 25 Years." *New York Times*, 28 April 2000: B2.

Rozen, Leah. "A Perfect Matchup for a Mystery Queen." *Good Housekeeping*, November 1996. EBSCOhost. On-line. 13 August 2001.

Siegel, Micki. "Mother Knows Best!" *Good Housekeeping*, May 1995. EBSCOhost. On-line. 13 August 2001.

Stasio, Marilyn. "Dressed to Kill in the World of Fashion." *New York Times*, 12 January 1997: Television 6–7, 27.

Swanson, Jean, and Dean James. "Clark, Mary Higgins." In *By a Woman's Hand: A Guide to Mystery Fiction by Women*. New York: Berkeley Books, 1994: 45–46.

Toepfer, Susan. "A Clean-Cut Case." *People*, 27 May 1996: 36.

"What the World Is Reading." *Economist*, 17 July 1999. EBSCOhost. On-line. 13 August 2001.

Whissen, Thomas. "Mary Higgins Clark." In *Great Women Mystery Writers: Classic to Contemporary*. Ed. Kathleen Gregory Klein. Westport, Conn.: Greenwood Press, 1994: 66–69.

"Writer Says Life Has Its Own Plot." *New York Times*, 18 May 1997: 31.

INTERVIEWS WITH MARY HIGGINS CLARK

Clark, Mary Higgins. Personal interview. New York, NY. 12 December 1994.

Clark, Mary Higgins. "Interrogating Mary." On-line. 22 April 2002 <http://www.simonsays.com/mhclark.html>

"An Interview with Mary Higgins Clark." In *Loves Music, Loves to Dance*. New York: Pocket Books, 1992: n.p.

MARY HIGGINS CLARK WEB SITE

http://www.simonsays.com/mhclark.html

REVIEWS AND CRITICISM

The Anastasia Syndrome and Other Stories (1989)

Booklist, 1 November 1989: 524.

Kent, Bill. Review of *The Anastasia Syndrome. New York Times Book Review*, 3 December 1989: 20.

Kirkus Review, 15 September 1989: 1348.

Los Angeles Times Book Review, 3 March 1991: 10.

Mitgang, Herbert. "An Escape from the Present." *New York Times*, 6 December 1989: Sec. 3, 25.

Publishers Weekly, 8 February 1991: 55.

Steinberg, Sybil. Review of *The Anastasia Syndrome. Publishers Weekly*, 29 September 1989: 61.

Toepfer, Susan. "Picks and Pans." *People*, 29 January 1990: 28.

The Lottery Winner: Alvirah and Willy Stories (1994)

Melton, Emily. Review of *The Lottery Winner. Booklist*, 15 October 1994: 370.

Steinberg, Sybil. Review of *The Lottery Winner. Publishers Weekly*, 17 October 1994: 62.

Silent Night (1995)

Nathan, Paul. "More of Mary." *Publishers Weekly*, 13 November 1995: 21.

Moonlight Becomes You (1996)

Stasio, Marilyn. "Crime." *New York Times Book Review*, 5 May 1996: 29.

Theiss, Terri. "The *Monitor*'s Guide to Bestsellers." *Christian Science Monitor*, 16 May 1996. On-line. EBSCOhost. 13 August 2001.

My Gal Sunday (1996)

Elias, Justine. Review of *My Gal Sunday. New York Times Book Review*, 15 December 1996: 25.

Pretend You Don't See Her (1997)

Marlowe, Kimberly B. Review of *Pretend You Don't See Her. New York Times Book Review*, 29 June 1997: 21.

Toefper, Susan. "Picks & Pans." *People*, 19 May 1997. EBSCOhost. On-line. 13 August 2001.

You Belong to Me (1998)

Bautz, Mark. Review of *You Belong to Me*. *People*, 27 April 1998. EBSCOhost. On-line. 13 August 2001.
Stasio, Marilyn. "Crime." *New York Times Book Review*, 19 April 1998: 30.

All Through the Night: A Suspense Story (1998)

Sanz, Cynthia. "Picks & Pans." *People*, 26 October 1998. EBSCOhost. On-line. 13 August 2001.
Williams, Wilda. "Fictional Stocking Stuffers." *Library Journal*, 1 November 1998. EBSCOhost. On-line. 13 August 2001.

We'll Meet Again (1999)

Arana, Marie. "Mary Higgins Clark: Queen of Suspense." *Washington Post Book World*, 18 April 1999: X08.
McLarin, Jenny. "New Mystery Reviews." *Booklist*, 14 April 1999: 1468.
Stasio, Marilyn. "Crime." *New York Times Book Review*, 23 May 1999: 33.

Before I Say Good-Bye (2000)

Jenish, D'Arcy, and Barbara Wickens. "Amazing Escapades." *Maclean's*, 17 July 2000. EBSCOhost. On-line. 13 August 2001.
Stasio, Marilyn. "Crime." *New York Times Book Review*, 16 April 2000: 32.

Deck the Halls (2000)

Flamm, Matthew. Review of *Deck the Halls*. *New York Times Book Review*, 14 January 2001: 19.
Review of *Deck the Halls*. *Publishers Weekly*, 30 October 2000: 47.
Wulff, Jennifer. "Picks & Pans." *People*, 18 December 2000. EBSCOhost. On-line. 29 January 2001.
Zvirin, Stephanie. "Upfront: Advance Reviews." *Booklist*, 1 November 2000: 492.

On the Street Where You Live (2001)

"Behind the Bestsellers." *Publishers Weekly*, 10 May 2001: 21.
Huntley, Kristine. "Upfront: Advance Reviews." *Booklist*, 14 April 2001: 1508.
Sanz, Cynthia. "Picks & Pans." *People*, 14 May 2001. EBSCOhost. On-line. 13 August 2001.

Toevs, Anne. "The *Monitor*'s Guide to Hardcover Fiction Bestsellers." *Christian Science Monitor,* 10 May 2001. EBSCOhost. On-line. 13 August 2001.

OTHER SECONDARY SOURCES

Aiken, Joan. "Plot and Character in Suspense Fiction." In *The Writer's Handbook.* Ed. Sylvia K. Burack. Boston: The Writer, 1991: 245–51.

Berger, Arthur Asa. *Cultural Criticism: A Primer of Key Concepts.* Foundations of Popular Culture, Vol. 4. Thousand Oaks, Calif.: Sage Publications, 1995.

Bertens, Hans. *Literary Theory: The Basics.* London: Routledge, 2001.

Cawelti, John G. *Adventure, Mystery, and Romance: Formula Stories as Art and Popular Culture.* Chicago: University of Chicago Press, 1976.

Klein, Kathleen Gregory. "Introduction." In *Great Women Mystery Writers: Classic to Contemporary.* Ed. Kathleen Gregory Klein. Westport, Conn.: Greenwood Press, 1994: 1–9.

Showalter, Elaine. "The Feminist Critical Revolution." In *The New Feminist Criticism: Essays on Women, Literature, and Theory.* Ed. Elaine Showalter. London: Virago Press, 1986: 3–17.

Symons, Julian. *Bloody Murder: From the Detective Story to the Crime Novel.* New York: Penguin, 1985.

Index

About the Author

LINDA DE ROCHE is Professor of English at Wesley College in Dover, Delaware. A specialist in American Literature, her publications include *Mary Higgins Clark: A Critical Companion* (Greenwood 1995), *Eric Segal: A Critical Companion* (Greenwood 1997) and *A Student Companion to F. Scott Fitzgerald* (Greenwood 2000).

Critical Companions to Popular Contemporary Writers
First Series—*also available on CD-ROM*

V. C. Andrews *by E. D. Huntley*

Tom Clancy *by Helen S. Garson*

Mary Higgins Clark *by Linda C. Pelzer*

Arthur C. Clarke *by Robin Anne Reid*

James Clavell *by Gina Macdonald*

Pat Conroy *by Landon C. Burns*

Robin Cook *by Loreena Laura Stookey*

Michael Crichton *by Elizabeth A. Trembley*

Howard Fast *by Andrew Macdonald*

Ken Follett *by Richard C. Turner*

John Grisham *by Mary Beth Pringle*

James Herriot *by Michael J. Rossi*

Tony Hillerman *by John M. Reilly*

John Jakes *by Mary Ellen Jones*

Stephen King *by Sharon A. Russell*

Dean Koontz *by Joan G. Kotker*

Robert Ludlum *by Gina Macdonald*

Anne McCaffrey *by Robin Roberts*

Colleen McCullough *by Mary Jean DeMarr*

James A. Michener *by Marilyn S. Severson*

Anne Rice *by Jennifer Smith*

Tom Robbins *by Catherine E. Hoyser and Lorena Laura Stookey*

John Saul *by Paul Bail*

Erich Segal *by Linda C. Pelzer*

Gore Vidal *by Susan Baker and Curtis S. Gibson*